MY SECRETS OF DAY TRADING IN STOCKS

RICHARD D. WYCKOFF

REPRINTED BY ANCIENT WISDOM PUBLICATIONS

WOODLAND, CALIFORNIA

Contents

My Secrets of Day trading Stocks
RICHARD D. WYCKOFF
Publisher information
ISBN-10 1234567890
ISBN-13 9780982499443

Foreword

Functioning as a trader and educator in the stock, commodity and bond markets throughout the early 1900s, Wyckoff was curious about the logic behind market action. Through conversations, interviews and research of the successful traders of his time, Wyckoff augmented and documented the methodology he traded and taught. Wyckoff worked with and studied them all, himself, Jesse Livermore, E. H. Harriman, James R. Keene, Otto Kahn, J.P. Morgan, and many other large operators of the day.

Wyckoff implemented his methods outlined in this book, in the financial markets, and grew his account to such a magnitude that he eventually owned nine and a half acres and a mansion next door to the General Motors' Industrialist, Alfred Sloan's Estate, in Great Neck, New York (Hamptons).

As Wyckoff became wealthier, he also became altruistic about the public's Wall Street experience. He turned his attention and passion to education, teaching, and in publishing exposés such as "Bucket shops and How to Avoid Them", which were run in New York's *The Saturday Evening Post* starting in 1922.

CHAPTER ONE

Introduction

THERE is a widespread demand for more light on the subject of Tape Reading or the reading of moment by moment transactions in a stock.

Thousands of those who operate in the stock market now recognize the fact that the market momentarily indicates its own immediate future, and that these indications are accurately recorded in the market transactions second by second, and therefore those who can interpret what transactions take place second by second or moment by moment have a distinct advantage over the general trading public.

Such an opinion is warranted, for it is well known that many of the most successful traders of the present day began as Tape Readers, trading in small lots of stock with a capital of only a few hundred dollars. Joe Manning, was one of the shrewdest and most successful of all the traders on the floor of the New York Stock Exchange.

A friend of mine once said: "Joe and I used to trade in ten share lots together. He was an ordinary trader, just like me. We used to hang over the same ticker." The speaker was, at the time he made the remark, still trading in ten-share lots, while I happened to know that Joe's bank balance -- his active working capital -- amounted to $100,000, and that this represented but a part of the fortune built on his ability to understand the tapes' secrets and interpret the language of the tape. Why was one of these men able to generate a fortune, while the other never acquired more than a few thousand dollars day trading?

Their chances were equal at the start of their pursuit as far as capital and opportunity. The profits were there, waiting to be won by either or both. The answer seems to be in the peculiar qualifications of the mind, highly potent in the successful trader, but not possessed by the other. There is, of course, an element of luck in every case, but pure luck could not be so sustained in Manning's case as to carry him through day trading operations covering a term of years.

The famous Jesse Livermore used to trade solely on what the tape told him, closing out every-thing before the close of the market. He traded from an office and paid the regular commissions, yet three trades out of five showed profits. Having made a fortune, he invested it in bonds and gave them all to his wife. Anticipating the 1907 panic, he put his $13,000 automobile up for a loan of $5,000, and with this capital started to play the bear side of the market, using his profits as additional margin. At one time he was short 70,000 shares of Union Pacific stock. His whole lot was covered on one of the panic days, and his net profits were over a million dollars!

By proper mental qualifications we do not mean the mere ability to take a loss, define the trend, or to execute some other move characteristic of the professional trader. I refer to the active or dormant qualities in his make-up. For example: The power to force himself into the right mental attitude before trading; to control his emotions: fear, anxiety, elation, recklessness; and to train his mind into obedience so that it recognizes but one master - the tape. These qualities are as vital as natural ability, or what is called the sixth sense in trading. Some people are born musicians, others seemingly void of musical taste, develop themselves until they become virtuosos.

Jacob Field is another exponent of Tape Reading. Those who knew "Jakey" when he began his Wall Street career, noted his ability to read the tape and follow the trend. His talent for this work was doubtless born in him, time and experience have proven and intensified it. Whatever awards James R. Keene won as operator or syndicate manager, do not detract from his reputation as a Tape Reader as well. His scrutiny of the tape was so intense that he appeared to be in a trance while his mental processes were being worked out. He seemed to analyze prices, volumes and fluctuations down to the finest imaginable point. It was then his practice to telephone to the floor of the Stock Exchange to ascertain the character of the buying or selling and with this auxiliary information complete his judgment and make his commitments.

At his death Mr. Keene stood on the pinnacle of fame as a Tape Reader, his daily presence at the ticker hearing testimony that the work paid and paid well.

You might be urged to say: "Yes, but these are rare examples. The average man or woman never makes a success of day trading by reading moment by moment transactions of the market." Right you are! The average man or woman seldom makes a success of anything! That is true of trading stocks, business endeavours or even hobbies! Success in day trading usually results from years of painstaking effort and absolute concentration upon the subject.

It requires the devotion of one's whole time and attention to - the tape. He should have no other business or profession. "A man cannot serve two masters," and the tape is a tyrant. One cannot become a Tape Reader by giving the ticker absent treatment, nor by running into his broker's office after lunch, or seeing "how the market closed" from his evening newspaper. He cannot study this art from the far end of a telephone wire. He should spend twenty-seven hours a week or more at a ticker, and many more hours away from it studying his mistakes and finding the "why" of his losses.

If Tape Reading were an exact science, one would simply have to assemble the factors, carry out the operations indicated, and trade accordingly. But the factors influencing the market are infinite in their number and character, as well as in their effect upon the market, and to attempt the construction of a Tape Reading formula would seem to be futile. However, something of the kind (in the rough) may develop as we progress in this investigation, so kind an open mind because we have many secrets, tricks and tips to reveal that are not in the pocket of the average day trader.

WHAT IS TAPE READING?

This question may be best answered by first deciding what it is not.

Tape Reading is not merely looking at the tape to determine how prices are running.

It is not reading the news and then buying or selling "if the stock acts right."

It is not trading on tips, opinions, or information.

It is not buying "because they look strong," or selling "because they look weak."

It is not trading on chart indications or by other mechanical methods.

It is not "buying on dips and selling on peaks."

Nor is it any of the hundred other foolish things practiced by the millions of people without method, planning or strategy.

It seems to us, based on our experience, that Tape Reading is the defined science of determining from the tape the immediate trend of prices. It is a method of forecasting, from what appears on the tape now in the moment, what is likely to appear in the immediate future. Tape Reading is rapid-fire common sense. Its object is to determine whether stocks are being accumulated or distributed, marked up or down, or whether they are being neglected by the large investors.

The Tape Reader aims to make deductions from each succeeding transaction - every shift of the market kaleidoscope, to grasp a new situation, force it, lightning-like, through the weighing machine of the mind, and to reach a decision which can be acted upon with coolness and precision. It is gauging the momentary supply and demand in particular stocks and in the whole market, comparing the forces behind each and their relationship, each to the other and to all.

A day trader is like the manager of a department store; into his office are submitted hundreds of reports of sales made by the various departments. He notes the general trend of business - whether demand is heavy or light throughout the store, but lends special attention to the products in which demand is abnormally strong or weak.

When he finds it difficult to keep his shelves full in a certain department or of a certain product, he instructs his buyers accordingly, and they increase their buying orders for that product; when certain products do not move he knows there is little demand (or a market) for them, therefore, he lowers his prices (seeking a market) to induce more purchases by his customers.

A floor trader on the exchange who stands in one crowd all day is like the buyer for one department in a store - he sees more quickly than anyone else the demand for that type of product, but has no way of comparing it to what may have strong or weak demand in other parts of the store.

He may be trading on the long side of Union Pacific stock, which has a strong upward trend, when suddenly a decline in another stock will demoralize the market for Union Pacific stock, and he will be forced to compete with others who have stocks to sell.

The Tape Reader, on the other hand, from his perch at

the ticker, enjoys a bird's eye view of the whole field. When serious weakness develops in any quarter, he is quick to note the changes taking place, weigh them and act accordingly.

Another advantage in favour of the Tape Reader: The tape tells the news minutes, hours and days before the newspapers, and before it can become current gossip. Everything from a foreign war to the elimination of a dividend; from a Supreme Court decision to the ravages of the boll-weevil is reflected primarily upon the tape.

The insider who knows a dividend is to be jumped from 6 per cent to 10 per cent shows his hand on the tape when he starts to accumulate the stock, and the investor with 100 shares to sell makes his fractional impress upon its market price.

The market is like a slowly revolving wheel. Whether the wheel will continue to revolve in the same direction, stand still or reverse depends entirely upon the forces which come in contact with its hub and tread. Even when the contact is broken, and nothing remains to affect its course, the wheel retains a certain impulse from the most recent dominating force, and revolves until it comes to a standstill or is subjected to other influences.

The element of manipulation need not discourage anyone. Manipulators are giant traders, with deep pockets. The trained ear can detect the steady "chomp, chomp," as they gobble up stocks, and their teeth marks are recognized in the fluctuations and the quantities of stock appearing on the tape. Little traders are at liberty to tiptoe wherever the food trail leads, but they must be careful that the giants do not turn quickly on them. The Tape Reader has many advantages over the long-term investor. He never ventures far from shore; that is he plays with a close stop, never laying himself open to a large loss. Accidents or catastrophes cannot seriously injure him because he can reverse his position in an instant, and follow the newly-formed stream from source to mouth. As his position on either the long or short side is confirmed and emphasized, he increases his line, thus following up the advantage gained.

A pure tape reading day trader does not care to carry stocks over night. The tape is then silent, and he only knows what to do when it tells him. Something may occur at midnight which may crumple up his diagram of the next day's market. He leaves nothing to chance; hence he prefers a clean sheet when the market gong strikes. By this method interest charges on margin are avoided, reducing the percentage against him to a considerable extent.

The Tape Reader is like a vendor of fruit who, each morning, provides himself with a stock of the choicest and most seasonable products, and for which there is the greatest demand. He pays his cash and disposes of the goods as quickly as possible, at a profit varying from 50 to 100 per cent on cost. To carry his stock over night causes a loss on account of spoilage. This corresponds with the interest charge to the trader.

The fruit vendor is successful because he knows what and when to buy, also where and how to sell. But there are stormy days when he cannot go out; when buyers do not appear; when he is arrested, fined, or locked up by a blue coated despot or his wares are scattered abroad by a careless trackmen. All of these unforeseen circumstances are a part of trading and life, in general.

Wall Street will readily apply these situations to the various attitudes in which the Tape Reader finds himself. He ventures $100 to make $200, and as the market goes in his favour his risk is reduced, but there are times when he finds himself at sea, with his stock deteriorating. Or the market is so unsettled that he does not know how to act; he is caught on stop or held motionless in a dead market; he takes a series of losses, or is obliged to be away from the tape when opportunities occur. His calculations are completely upset by some unforeseen event or his capital is impaired by overtrading or poor judgment. The vendor does not hope to buy a barrel of apples for $3 and sell them the same day for $300. He expects to make from nothing to $3 a day. He depends upon a small but certain profit, which will average enough over a week or a month to pay him for his time and labour.

This is the objective point of the Tape Reader - to make an average profit. In a month's operations he may make $4,000 and lose $3,000 - a net profit of $1,000 to show for his work. If he can keep this average up, trading in 100 share lots, throughout a year, he has only to increase his unit to 200, 300, and 500 shares or more, and the results will be tremendous.

The amount of capital or the size of the order is of secondary importance to this question: Can you trade in and out of all kinds of markets and show an average profit over losses, commissions, etc.? If so, you are getting proficient in the art of tape reading. If you can trade with only a small average loss per day, or come out even, you are rapidly getting there. A Tape Reader abhors information and follows a definite and thoroughly tested plan, which, after months and years of practice, becomes second nature to him. His mind forms habits that operate automatically in guiding his market adventures. Practice will make the Tape Reader just as proficient in forecasting stock market events, but his intuition will be reinforced by logic, reason and analysis.

Here we find the characteristics that distinguish the Tape Reader from the Scalper. The latter is essentially one who tries to grab a point or two profit "without rhyme or reason" - he doesn't care how, so long as he gets it. A Scalper will trade on a news tip, a look, a guess, a hear-say, gossip - on what he thinks or what a friend of a friend of friend says.

The Tape Reader evolves himself into a 'trading machine' which takes note of a situation, weighs it, decides upon a course and gives an order. There is no acceleration of the pulse, no nervousness, no hopes or fears concerning his actions. The result produces neither elation nor depression: there is calmness before, during and after the trade.

The Scalper is a car without shocks, bouncing over every little bump in the road with rattling windows, a rickety motion and a strong tendency to swerve into oncoming traffic.

The Tape Reader, on the other hand, is like a fine train, which travels smoothly and steadily along the tracks of the tape, acquiring direction and speed from the market engine, and being influenced by nothing else whatever.

Having thus described our ideal Tape Reader in a general way, let us inquire into some of the pre-requisite qualifications.

First, he must be absolutely self-reliant and self-determining. A dependent person, whose judgment hangs on the advise or passing words of others will find himself swayed by a thousand outside influences. At critical points his judgment will be useless because he has not been able to exercise his 'judgment muscles' – they are weak from inactivity! The professional day trader must be able to say: "The facts are in front of me; my analysis of the situation is this; therefore I will do this and this."

Second, he must be familiar with the mechanics of the market, so that every little incident affecting prices will be given due weight. He should know the history of earnings of the stocks he is trading and financial condition of the companies in whose stock he is trading; the ways in which large operators accumulate and distribute stocks; the different kinds of markets (bull, bear, sideways, trending, etc.); be able to measure the effect of news and rumours; know when and in what stocks it is best to trade and measure the market forces behind them; know when to cut a loss (without fear or depression) and take a profit (without pride and puffery).

He must study the various swings and know where the market and the various stocks stand; he must recognize the inherent weakness or strength in prices; understand the basis or logic of movements. He should recognize the turning points of the market; see in his mind's eye what is happening on the floor of the exchange.

He must have the nerve to stand a series of losses; persistence to keep him at the work or trading during adverse periods; self-control to avoid overtrading; an amiable and calm disposition to balance him at all times.

For perfect concentration as a protection from stock tips, gossip and other influences which are rampant in a broker's office he should, if possible, seclude himself. A small room with a ticker, a desk and private telephone connection with his broker's office are all the facilities required. The work requires such delicate balance of the faculties that the slightest influence either way may throw the result against the trader. You may say: "Nothing influences me," but unconsciously it does affect your judgment to know that another man is bearish at a point where he thinks stocks should be bought. The mere thought, "He may be right," has a deterrent influence upon you and clouds your own judgments; you hesitate and the opportunity is lost. No matter how the market goes from that point, you have missed a beat and your mental machinery is thrown out of gear.

Silence and concentration, therefore, is needed to lubricate the day trader's mind. The advisability of having even a news feed in the room, is a subject for discussion. The conclusion is that 'news' is 'news'; the recording of what has already taken place, no more, no less. It announces the cause for the effect that has already been more or less felt in the market. On the other hand the tape tells the present and future of the market. Money is made in Tape Reading by anticipating what is coming - not by waiting till it happens and going with the crowd.

The effect of news is an entirely different proposition. Considerable light is thrown on the technical strength or weakness of the market and special stocks by their action in the face of important news. For the moment it seems to us that a news feed might be admitted to the sanctum, provided its whisperings are given only the weight to which they are entitled.

To evolve a practical methodology – one which the trader may use in his daily operations and which those with varying proficiency in the art of Tape Reading will find of value and assistance - such is the task we have set before us in this manual. We shall consider all the market factors of vital importance in Tape Reading, as well as methods used by experts. These will be illustrated by reproductions from the tape. Every effort will be made to produce something of definite, tangible value to those who are now operating in a hit-or-miss sort of way.

CHAPTER TWO
Getting Started In Tape Reading

WHEN embarking on any new business enterprise, the first thing to consider is the amount of capital required.

To study Tape Reading "on paper" is one thing, but to practice and become proficient in the art is quite another. Almost anyone can make money on imaginary trades because there is no risk of any kind - the mind is free from the strain and apprehension that accompanies an actual trade; fear does not enter into the situation; patience is unlimited.

All this is changed when even a small commitment is made. Then his judgment becomes warped, and he closes the trade in order to get mental relief. As these are all symptoms of inexperience they cannot be overcome by avoiding the issue. The business-like thing to do is to wade right into the game and learn to play it under conditions that are to be met and conquered before success can be attained.

After a complete absorption of every available piece of educational writing bearing upon Tape Reading, it is best to commence trading in ten share lots, so as to acquire genuine trading experience. This may not suit some people with a propensity for gambling, and who look upon the ten-share trader as being afraid and a 'babe in the woods'. The average lamb with $10,000 in capital wants to commence with 500 to

1000 share lots - he wishes to start at the top and work down. It is only a question of time when he will have to trade in 50 share lots – having lost the majority of his capital in large trades. To us it seems better to start at the bottom with 50 shares. There is plenty of time in which to increase the unit if you are successful. If success is not eventually realized you will be many dollars better off for having risked a minimum quantity. It has already been shown by experience that the market for odd lots (100 shares or less) on the exchanges is very active, so there is no other excuse for the novice who desires to trade in round lots than greed-of-gain, or a get-rich-quick mentality. Think of a baby, just learning to walk, being entered in a race with professional sprinters! In the previous chapter we suggested that success in Tape Reading should be measured by the number of points profit over points lost.

For all practical purposes, therefore, we might trade 10 share lots, were there no objection on the part of our broker and if this quantity were not so absurdly small as to invite careless execution. 50 shares is really the smallest quantity that should be considered, but we mention shares simply to impress upon our readers that in studying Tape Reading, it's better to keep in mind that you are playing for points, not dollars. The dollars will come along fast enough if you can make more points net than you lose. The professional billiards player playing for a stake aims to out-point his antagonist. After trading for a few months don't consider the dollars you are ahead or behind, but analyze the record in points. In this way your progress can be studied.

As the initial losses in trading are likely to be heavy, and as the estimated capital must be a more or less an arbitrary amount, we should say that units of $5,000 would be necessary for each 50 share lot traded in at the beginning. This allows for more losses than profits, and leaves a margin with which to proceed. Some people will secure a footing with less capital; others may he obliged to put up several units of $5,000 each before they begin to show profits; still others will spend a fortune (large or small) without making it pay, or meeting with any encouragement.

Look over the causes of failure of most businesses and you will find the chief causes to be: 1) Lack of capital, and 2) Incompetence. Lack of capital in Wall Street trading can usually be traced to over-trading. This proves the saying, "Over-trading is financial suicide." It may mean too large a quantity of stock being traded, or if the trader loses money, he may not reduce the size of his trade to correspond with the shrinkage in his capital.

To make our point clear: A man starts trading in 50 share lots with $1,000 capital. After a series of losses he finds that he has only $500 remaining. That's on 10 points on 50 shares, but does he reduce his orders in shares? No. He risks the $500 on a 50 share trade in a last desperate effort to recoup. The stock loses 10 points and he's out $500.

After being wiped out he tells his friends how he

"could have made money if be had had more capital." Incompetence really deserves first place in the list. Supreme ignorance is the predominant feature of both stock market lamb and seasoned speculator.

It is surprising how many people stay in the Street year after year, acquiring nothing more, apparently, than a keen scent for tips and gossip. Ask them a technical question that smacks of method and planning in trading and they are unable to reply. Such folks remain on the Street for one of two reasons: They have either been "lucky" or their margins are replenished from some source outside of the markets. The proportion of commercial failures due to Lack of Capital or Incompetence is about 60 per cent. Call the former by its Wall Street cognomen – Overtrading - and the percentage of stock market disasters traceable thereto would be about 90 per cent. Success is only for the few who really want the work (not the glory), and the problem is to ascertain, with the minimum expenditure of time and money, whether you are fitted for the work.

These, in a nutshell, are the vital questions up to this point:

Have you technical knowledge of the market and the factors that move it?

Have you $1,000 or more that you can afford to lose in an effort to demonstrate your ability at day trading?

Can you devote your entire time and attention to the study and the practice of this science?

Are you so fixed financially that you are not dependent

upon your possible profits, and so that you will not suffer if none are forthcoming now or later?

There is no sense in mincing words over this matter, nor in holding out false encouragement to people who are looking for an easy, drop-a-penny-in-the-slot way of making money. Tape Reading is hard work, and those who are mentally lazy need not apply. Nor should anyone to whom it will mean worry as to where his bread and butter is coming from. Money-worry is not conducive to clearheadedness. Over-anxiety upsets the equilibrium of a trader more than anything else. So, if you cannot afford the time and money, and have not the other necessary qualifications, do not begin. Start right or not at all.

Having decided to proceed, the trader who is equal to the foregoing finds himself asking, "Where shall I trade?"

The choice of a broker is an important matter to the Tape Reader. He should find one especially equipped for the work: who can give close attention to his orders, furnish quick bid and ask prices, and other technical information, such as the quantities wanted and offered at different levels, etc.

The broker most to be desired should never have so much business on hand that he cannot furnish the trader with a verbal flash of what "the crowd" in this or that stock is doing. This is important, for at times it will be money in the pocket to know just in what momentary position a stock or the whole market stands. The broker who is not overburdened with business can give this service; he can also devote time and care to the execution of orders.

Let me give an instance of how this works out in practice: You are long 100 shares of Union stock, with a stop-order just under the market price; a dip comes and 100 shares sells at your stop price - say 164. Your careful, and not too busy broker, stands in the crowd. He observes that several thousand shares are bid for at 164 and only a few hundred are offered at the price. He does not sell the stock, but waits to see if it won't rally. It does rally. You are given a new lease of life. This handling of the order may benefit you $50, $100 or several hundred dollars in each instance, and is an advantage to be sought when choosing a broker. Having knowledge of the depth of the market – how much is offered for sale and at what price and how much is bid and at what price; the placement of bid and ask orders are of tremendous importance to the tape reader.

The brokerage house which transacts an active commission business for a large clientele is unable to give this type of service. Its stop-orders and other orders not "close to the market," must be given to exchange Specialists, and the press of business is such that it cannot devote marked attention to the orders of any one client.

In a small brokerage house, such as we have described, the Tape Reader is less likely to be bothered by a gallery of traders, with their diverse and loud-spoken opinions. In other words, he will be left more or less to himself and be free to concentrate upon his task. The ticker should he within calling distance of the telephone to the Stock Exchange. Some brokers have a way of making you or a clerk walk a mile to give an order. Every step means delay. The elapse of a few seconds may result in a lost market or opportunity.

If you are in a small private room away from the order desk, there should be a private telephone connecting you with the order clerk. Slow execution won't make it in Tape Reading. Your orders should generally be given "at the market." We make this statement as a result of long experience and observation, and believe we can demonstrate the advisability of it. The process of reporting transactions on the tape, consumes from five seconds to five minutes, depending upon the activity of the market. For argument's sake, let us consider that the average interval between the time a sale takes place on the floor and the report appears on the tape is half a minute. A market order in an active stock is usually executed and reported to the customer in about two minutes. Half this time is consumed in putting your broker into the crowd with the order in hand; the other half in transmitting the report. Hence, when Union Pacific comes 164 on the tape and you instantly decide to buy it, the period of time between your decision and the execution of your order is as follows:

The tape is behind the market …30 seconds Time elapsed before broker can execute the order … 30 seconds It will therefore be seen that your decision is based on a price which prevailed half a minute ago, and that you must purchase if you will, at the price at which the stock stands one minute after. This might happen between your decision and the execution of your order: UP 164, ¼, 1/8, ¼, ½, ½, 3/8, ¼, 1/8, 164, ...and yours might be the last hundred. When the report arrives you may not be able to swear that it was bought at 164 before or after it touched 164½. Or you might get it at 164½, even though it was 164 when you gave the order, and when the report was handed to you. Just as often, the opposite will take place - the stock will go in your favour. In fact, the thing averages up in the long run, so that traders who do not give market orders are hurting their own chances.

An infinite number of traders seeing Union Pacific at 164, will say: "Buy me a hundred at 164." The broker who is not too busy will go into the crowd, and, finding the stock at 164¼ at ¼ will report back to the office that "Union is ¼ bid." The trader gives his broker no credit for this service; instead he considers it a sign that his broker, the floor traders and the insiders have all conspired to make him pay ¼ per cent higher for his 100 shares, so he replies: "Let it stand at 164. If they don't give it to me at that, I won't buy it at all." How foolish! Yet it is characteristic of the style of reasoning used by the public. His argument is that the stock, for good and sufficient reasons, is a purchase at 164. At 164¼ or 1/2 these reasons are completely nullified; the stock becomes dear, or he cares more to foil the plans of this "band of robbers" than for a possible profit. If you believe UP stock is cheap at 164 it's still cheap at 164¼. Here's the best advice I can give: If you can't trust your broker, get another.

If you think the law of supply and demand is altered to catch your $25, floor - you better reorganize your thinking. Were you on the floor you could probably buy at 164 the minute it touched that figure, but even then you have no certainty. You would, however, be 60 seconds nearer to the market. Your commission charges would also be practically eliminated.

Therefore, if you have two hundred seventy or eighty thousand dollars which you do not especially need, buy a seat on the Stock Exchange. A Tape Reader who deserves the name, makes money in spite of commissions, taxes and delays. If you don't get aboard your train, you'll never arrive.

Giving limited orders loses more good dollars than it saves. We refer, of course, to orders in the big, active stocks, wherein the bid and ask prices are usually 1/8th apart. Especially is this true in closing out a trade. Many foolish people are interminably hung up because they try to save eighths by giving limited orders in a market that is running away from them. For the Tape Reader there is a psychological moment when he must open or close his trade. His orders must therefore be "at the market." Haggling over fractions will make him lose the thread of the tape, upset his poise and interrupt the workings of his mental machinery.

In 'scale' buying or selling it is obvious that limit orders must be used. There are certain other times when they are of advantage, but as the Tape Reader generally goes with the trend, it is a case of "get on or get left." By all means "get on."

The selection of stocks is an important matter, and should be decided in a general way before one starts to trade. Let us see what we can reason out.

If you are trading in 100 share lots, your stock must move your way one point to make $100 profit. Which class of stocks are most likely to move a point? Answer: The higher priced issues. Looking over the records we find that a stock selling around $150 will average 2½ points fluctuations a day, while one selling at 50 will average only one point. Consequently, you have 2½ times more action in the higher priced stock. The commission and tax charges are the same in both. Interest charges are three times as large, but this is an insignificant item to the Tape Reader who doses out his trades each day.

The higher priced stocks also cover a greater number of points during the year or cycle than those of lower price. Stocks like Great Northern, although enjoying a much wider range, are not desirable for trading purposes when up to 300 or more, because fluctuations and bid and asked prices are too far apart to permit rapid in-and-out trading. Look for stock leaders where there is a large floating supply; where there is a wide public interest in the stock; where there is a broad market and wide swings; where trends are definable (not too erratic); these are popular with floor traders, big and little. It is better for a Tape Reader to trade in one or two stocks at the most - rather than more - since concentration is absolutely necessary for the work at hand.

Stocks have habits and characteristics that are as distinct as those of human beings or animals. By a close study the trader becomes intimately acquainted with these habits and is able to anticipate the stock's action under given circumstances. A stock may be stubborn, sensitive, irresponsive, complaisant, and aggressive; it may dominate the tape or trail along behind the rest; it is whimsical and exhibit serendipity. Its moods must be studied if you would know it personally. Study implies concentration. A person who trades in a dozen stocks at a time cannot concentrate on one.

The popular method of trading (which means the unsuccessful way) is to say: "I think the market's going bearish. 'Smelters', 'Copper' and 'St. Paul' have had the biggest rise lately; they ought to have a good reaction; sell a hundred short of each for me." Trades based on what one "thinks" seldom pan out well. The selection of two or three stocks by guesswork, instead of one by reason and analysis, explains many of the public's losses. If a trader wishes to trade in three hundred shares, let him sell that quantity of this stock which he knows most about.

Unless he is playing the long term he injures his chances by trading in several stocks at once. It's like chasing a drove of pigs - while you're watching this one the others get away. It's better to concentrate on one or two stocks and study them exhaustively. You will find that what applies to one does not always fit the other; each must be judged on its own merits. The varying price levels, volumes, percentage of floating supply, earnings, the manipulation of large traders and other factors, all tend to produce a different combination in each particular case.

CHAPTER THREE
Analyzing The List of Stocks

IN the last chapter we referred to Union Pacific stock as the most desirable stock for active trading.

A friend of mine once made a composite chart of the principal active stocks, for the purpose of ascertaining which, in its daily fluctuations, followed the course of the general market most accurately. He found Union Pacific was what might be called the market backbone or leader, while the others, especially Reading Railroad, frequently showed erratic tendencies, running up or down, more or less contrary to the general trend. Of all the issues under inspection, none possessed the all-around steadiness and general desirability for trading purposes displayed by Union Pacific. But the Tape Reader, even if he decides to operate exclusively in one stock, cannot close his eyes to what is going on in others.

Frequent opportunities occur elsewhere. In proof of this, take the market in the early fall of 1907: Union Pacific was the leader throughout the rise from below 150 to 167 5/8. For three or four days before this advance culminated, heavy selling occurred in Reading, St. Paul, Copper, Steel and Smelters, under cover of the strength in Union. This made the turning point of the market as clear as daylight. One had only to go short of Reading and await the break, or he could have played Union with a close stop, knowing that the whole market would collapse as soon as Union turned downward.

When the liquidation in other stocks was completed, Union stopped advancing, the supporting orders were withdrawn, and the "pre-election break" took place. This amounted to over a 20 point decline in Union, with proportionate declines in the rest of the groups' list.

The operator who was watching only Union would have been surprised at this; but had he viewed the whole market he must have seen what was coming. Knowing the point of distribution, he would be on the lookout for the accumulation which must follow, or at least the level where support would be forthcoming. Had he been expert enough to detect this, quick money could have been made on the subsequent rally as well.

While certain stocks constitute the backbone or leadership position, this important member is only one part of the market body that, after all, is very like the physical structure of a human being. Suppose Union Pacific is strong and advancing. Suddenly New York Central develops an attack of weakness; Consolidated Gas starts a decline; American Ice becomes nauseatingly weak; Southern Railway and Great Western follow suit. There may be nothing the matter with the "leader," but its strength will be affected by weakness among all the others. A bad break may come in Brooklyn Rapid Transit, occasioned by a political attack, or other purely local influence. This cannot possibly affect the business of the large transportation stocks or transcontinentals, yet St. Paul, Union, and Reading decline as much as B. R. T.

A person whose finger is crushed will sometimes faint from the shock to his nervous system, although the injured member will not affect the other members or functions of the body. The time-worn illustration of the "chain which is as strong as its weakest link", will not serve. When the weak link breaks the chain is in two parts, each part being as strong as its weakest link. The market does not break in two, even when it receives a severe blow. If something occurs in the nature of a financial disaster, interest rates rise, investment demand falls, public sentiment or confidence is shaken, or corporate earning power is declining or are deeply affected - a tremendous break may occur, but there is always a level, even in a panic, where buying power becomes strong enough to produce a rally or a permanent upturn.

The Tape Reader must endeavour to operate in that stock which combines the widest swings with the broadest market; he may therefore frequently find it to his advantage to switch temporarily into other stock issues which seem to offer the quickest and surest profits. Therefore it is necessary for us to become familiar with the characteristics of the principal speculative methods that we may judge their advantages in this respect, as well as their weight and bearing upon a given market situation.

The market is made by the minds of many men. The state of these minds is reflected in the prices of securities in which their owners operate. Let's examine some of the individuals, as well as the influences behind certain stocks and groups of stocks in their various relationships. This will, in a sense, enable us to measure their respective power to affect the whole list or the specific issue in which we decide to operate. The market leaders are, at the time of this writing – and for illustration only -, Union Pacific, Reading, Steel, St. Paul, Anaconda and Smelters. Manipulators, professionals and the public derive their inspiration largely from the action of these six issues, in which, except during the "war" markets of 1914-16, from forty to eighty per cent of the total daily transactions are concentrated. We will therefore designate these as the "Big Six".

The Tape Reader should understand basic principles of the market. One being that leadership changes frequently. But for our purpose we will concentrate on this list. Three stocks out of the Big Six are chiefly influenced by the buying and selling operations of what is known as the Kuhn-Loeb-Standard Oil group. Their four stocks are Union, St. Paul, Reading and Anaconda. Of the other two, Smelters is handled by the Guggenheims, while Steel, controlled by Morgan, is unquestionably swung up and down more by the influence of public sentiment than anything else. Of course, the condition of the steel trade forms the basis of important movements in this issue, and occasionally Morgan or some other large interest may take a hand by buying or selling a few hundred thousand shares, but, generally speaking; it is the attitude of the public which chiefly affects the price of Steel common. This should be borne strictly in mind, as it is a valuable guide to the technical position of the market, which turns on the overbought or oversold condition of the market.

Next in importance comes what we will term the Secondary Leaders; for example those that at times burst into great activity, accompanied by large volume. These are termed Secondary Leaders, because while they seldom influence the

Big Six to a marked extent the less important issues usually fall into line at their initiative.

Another group which we will call the Minor Stocks is comprised of less important issues, mostly low-priced, and embracing many public favourites. Some people, when they see an advance inaugurated in some of the Minor Stocks, are led to buy the Primary or Secondary Leaders, on the ground that the latter will be bullishly affected. This sometimes occurs, more often it doesn't. It is just as foolish to expect a 5,000 share trader to follow the trading patterns of a 100 share trader, or a 100 share man to be influenced by buying and selling of the 10 share trader.

The various stocks in the market are like a gigantic fleet of boats, all hitched together and being towed by the tugs "Interest Rate," and "Business Conditions". In the first row are the Big Six; behind them, the Secondary Leaders, the Minors, and the Miscellaneous issues. It takes time to generate steam and to get the fleet under way. The leaders are first to feel the impulse; the others follow in turn.

Should the tugs halt, the fleet will run along for a while under its own momentum, and there will be a certain amount of bumping, hacking and filling. In case the direction of the tugs is changed abruptly, the bumping is apt to be severe. Obviously, those in the rear cannot gain and hold the leadership without an all-around readjustment.

The Leaders are representative of America's greatest industries - railroading, steel making, and mining. It is but natural that these stocks should form the principal outlet for the country's speculative tendencies. The Union Pacific and

St. Paul systems cover the entire West. Reading, of itself a large railroad property, dominates the coal mining industry; it is so interlaced with other railroads as to typify the Eastern situation. Steel is closely bound up with the state of general business throughout the states, while Anaconda and Smelters are the controlling factors in copper mining and the smelting industry. This is how you should look at groups of stocks. Who is the Primary Leader in the group? Who are the Secondary Leaders and who the Minor issues? By classifying the principal active stocks we can recognize more clearly the forces behind their movements.

For instance, if Consolidated Gas suddenly becomes strong and active, we know it will probably affect Brooklyn Union Gas, but there is no reason why the other stocks should advance more than slightly and out of sympathy. If all the stocks in the Standard Oil group advance in a steady and sustained fashion, we know that these capitalists are engaged in a bull campaign. As these people do not enter deals for a few points it is safe to go along with them for a while, or until distribution becomes apparent. An outbreak of speculation in Colorado Fuel is not necessarily a bull argument on the other Steel stocks. If it were based on trade conditions, U. S. Steel would be the first to feel the impetus – then it would radiate to the others. In selecting the most desirable stock out of the Kuhn-Loeb-Standard Oil group, for instance, the Tape Reader must consider whether conditions favour the greatest activity and volumes in the railroad or industrial stocks. In the former case, his choice would be Union Pacific or St. Paul; in the latter, Anaconda. Erie may come out of its rut (as it did during the summer of 1907, when it was selling around 24), and attain leadership among the low-priced stocks.

This indicates some important development in Erie; it does not foreshadow a rise in all the low-priced stocks. But if a strong rise starts in Union Pacific, and Southern Pacific and the others in the group follow consistently, the Tape Reader will get into the leader and stay with it. He will not waste time on Erie, for while it is moving up 5 points, Union Pacific may advance 10 or 15 points, provided it is a genuine move.

Many valuable deductions may be made by studying groupings of stocks. Experience has shown that when a rise commences in a Secondary Leader, the Leaders are about done in their advance and distribution is taking place, under protection of the strength in the Secondary stock and others in its class. Professional traders used to call these stocks "Indicators."

The absence of inside manipulation in a stock leaves the way open for pools to operate, and many of the moves that are observed in these groups are produced by a handful of floor or office operators, who, by joining hands and swinging large quantities of stock, are able to force their stock in the desired direction. For example, U.S. Steel is swayed by conditions in the steel trade, and the speculative temper of the general public, assisted occasionally by some insiders. No other stock on the list is such a true index of the attitude of the public, or the technical position of the market. Including those who own the stock out-right, and those who carry it on margin.

Reports of the steel trade are most carefully scrutinized, and the corporation's earnings and orders on hand minutely studied by thousands. This great public rarely sells its favourite short, but carries it on margin until a profit is secured, or until it is shaken or scared out in a violent decline. So, if the stock is strong under adverse news, we may infer that public holdings are strongly fortified, and that confidence is strong as well. If Steel displays more than its share of weakness, an untenable position of the public is indicated. At this point public sentiment becomes intensely bullish and spreads itself in the low-priced speculative shares. Insiders in the junior steel stocks take advantage of this and are able to advance and find a good market for their holdings. Stocks find their chief inspiration in the orders for cars, locomotives, etc., placed by the railroads. These orders are dependent upon general business conditions. Consequently, the equipment issues can seldom be expected to do more than follow the trend of prosperity or depression.

We should introduce ourselves to the principal speculative mediums and their families, each of which, upon closer acquaintance, seems to have a sort of personality. If we stand in a room with fifty or a hundred people, all of whom we know, as regards their chief motives and characteristics, we can form definite ideas as to their probable actions under a given set of circumstances. So it behoves the Tape Reader to acquaint himself with the most minute of details pertaining to these market identities, also with the habits, motives and methods of the men who make the principal moves on the Stock Exchange chess board.

CHAPTER FOUR
Trading Rules

WHEN a person contemplates an extensive trip, one of the first things taken into account is the expense involved.

In planning our excursion into the realms of day trading we must, therefore, carefully weigh the expenses, or fixed charges in trading.

Were there no expenses, making a profit would be far easier - profits would merely have to exceed losses.

Whether you are a member of the New York Stock Exchange or not, in actual trading - profits must exceed losses and expenses. These are incurred in every trade, whether it shows a gain or a loss They consist of:

Commissions

Invisible eighth (i.e. the difference between bid and ask price, assuming that you buy and sell at the market price)

Income Tax on sale

Exchange fees

In addition... interest if the trade is carried over night.

By purchasing a New York Stock Exchange seat, the commission can be reduced to $1 per hundred shares, if bought and sold the same day, or $3.12 if carried over night. This advantage is partly offset by interest on the cost of the seat, dues, assessments, etc.

The "invisible eighth" is a factor that no one - not even a member - can overcome. The bid and asked price is never less than an eighth apart. If the market is 45¼ to 3/8 when you buy, you will as a rule, pay 45 3/8. Were you to sell it would be at 45 ¼. This hypothetical difference follows you all through the trade and has been designated by the writer as the "invisible eighth". The Tape Reader who is a non-member of the exchange must, therefore, realize that the instant he gives an order to go long or short 100 shares, he has lost an eighth of a point. In order that he may not fool himself, he should add his commissions to his purchase price, or deduct them from his selling price immediately. People who boast of their profits usually forget to deduct expenses.

Yet it is this insidious item that frequently throws the net result over to the debit side. The expression is frequently heard, "I got out even, except for the commissions," the speaker evidently scorning such a trifling consideration. This sort of self-deception is ruinous, as will be seen by computing the fixed charges on a trade of 100 shares. Bear in mind that a loss of the commission on the first trade leaves double that amount-to be made on the second trade before a dollar of profit is secured.

It therefore appears that the Tape Reader's problem is not only to eliminate losses, but to cover his expenses as quickly as possible. If he has a couple of points profit in a long trade, there is no reason why he should let the stock run back below his net buying price. Here circumstances seem to call for a stop order, so that no matter what happens, he will not be compelled to pay out money.

This stop should not be thrust in when net cost is too close to the market price. A small reaction must be allowed for. A Tape Reader is essentially one who follows the immediate trend. An expert can readily distinguish between a change of trend and a simple, minor reaction.

When his mental barometer indicates a change he does not wait for a stop order to be caught, but cleans house or reverses his position in an instant. The stop order at net cost is, therefore, of advantage only in case of a reversal which is sudden and pronounced. A stop should also be placed if the operator is obliged to leave the tape for more than a moment, or if the ticker suddenly is out of order. While he has his eye on the tape the market will tell him what to do. The moment this condition does not exist he must act as he would if temporarily stricken blind - he must protect himself from forces which may attack him in the dark.

I know a trader who once bought 500 shares of Sugar and then went out to lunch. He paid 25 cents for what he ate, but on returning to the tape he found that the total cost of that lunch was $5,000 and 25 cents! He had left no stop order, Sugar went down ten points, and his broker sent him a margin call.

The ticker has a habit of becoming incoherent at the most critical points. Curse it as we may, it will resume printing intelligibly when the trouble is overcome - not before. As the loss of even a few quotations may be important, a stop should be placed at once and left in until the flow of prices is resumed.

If a trade is carried overnight, a stop should be entered against the possibility of accident to the market or the trader. An important event may develop before the next day's opening by which the stock will be violently affected. The trader may be taken ill, be delayed in arrival, or in some way be incapacitated. A certain allowance must be made for accidents of every kind.

As to where the stop should be placed under such conditions, this depends upon circumstances. The consensus of shrewd and experienced traders is in favour of two points maximum gross loss on any one trade. This is purely arbitrary, however. The Tape Reader knows, as a rule, what to do when he is at the tape, but if he is separated from the market by any contingency, he will he obliged to fall back upon the arbitrary stop.

A closer stop may be obtained by noting the "points of resistance" in a stock - the levels at which the market turns after a reaction. For example, if you are short at 130 and the stock breaks to 128, rallies to 129, and then turns down again, the point of resistance is 129. The more time it turns at 129 the stronger the case you have. In case of temporary absence or interruption to the service, a good stop would be 129¼ or 129¼. These "points of resistance" will be more fully discussed later.

If the operator wishes to use an automatic stop, a very good method is this: Suppose the initial trade is made with a one-point stop. For every ¼ pt. the stock moves in your favour, change the stop to correspond, so that the stop is never more nor less than one point away from the extreme market price. This gradually and automatically reduces the risk, and if the Tape Reader be at all skilful, his profits must exceed losses. As soon as the stop is thus raised to cover commissions, it would seem best not to make it automatic thereafter, but let the market develop its own stop or "signal" to get out.

One trouble with this kind of a stop is that it interferes with the free play of judgment. An illustration will explain why: A tall woman and a short man attempt to cross the street. An automobile approaches. The woman sees that there is ample time in which to cross, but he has her by the arm and being undecided himself backs and fills, first pushing, then pulling her by the arm until they finally return to the curb, after a narrow escape. Left to herself, she would have known exactly what to do. It is the same with the Tape Reader. He is hampered by an automatic stop. It is best that he be free to act as his judgment dictates, without feeling compelled by a prior resolution to act according to hard and fast rule.

There is another time when the stop order is of value to the Tape Reader, viz., when his indications are not clearly defined. The original commitment should, of course, be made only when the trend is positively indicated, but situations will develop when he will be uncertain whether to stand pat, close out, or reverse his position. At such a time it seems better to push the stop up to a point as close as possible to the market price, without choking off the trade. By this we mean a reasonable area should be allowed for temporary fluctuations. If the stock emerges from its uncertainty by going in the desired direction, the stop can be changed or cancelled. If its trend becomes adverse, the trade is automatically closed.

Fear, hesitation and uncertainty are deadly enemies of the Tape Reader. The chief cause of fear is over-trading. Therefore commitments should be no greater than can be borne by one's susceptibility thereto. Hesitation can be overcome by disciplined self-training. To observe a positive indication and not act upon it is fatal - more so in closing than in opening a trade. The appearance of a definite indication should be immediately followed by an order. Seconds are often more valuable than minutes. The Tape Reader is not the captain - he is the engineer who controls the machinery. The Tape is the pilot and the engineer must obey orders with promptness and precision.

We have defined a Tape Reader as one who follows the immediate trend. This means that he pursues the line of least resistance. He goes with the market - he does not buck it. The operator who opposes the immediate trend pits his judgment and his hundred or more shares against the world's supply or demand and the weight of its millions of shares. Armed with a broom, he is trying to keep at bay the incoming tide. When he goes with the trend, the forces of supply, demand and manipulation are working for and with him.

A market which swings within a radius of a couple of points cannot be said to have a trend, and is a good one for the Tape Reader to avoid. The reason is - unless he catches the extremes of the little swings, he cannot pay commissions, take occasional losses and come out ahead. No yacht can win in a dead calm. As it costs him nearly half a point to trade, each risk should contain a probable two or five points profit, or it is not justified.

A mechanical engineer, given the weight of an object, the force of the blow that strikes it, and the element through which it must pass, can figure approximately how far the object will be driven. So the Tape Reader, by gauging the impetus or the energy with which a stock starts and sustains a movement, decides whether it is likely to travel far enough to warrant his going with it - whether it will pay its expenses and remunerate him for his boldness. The ordinary speculator trading on tips gulps a point or two profit and disdains a loss, unless it is big enough to strangle him. The Tape Reader must do the opposite - he must cut out every possible eighth loss and search for chances to make three, five and ten points. He does not have to grasp everything that looks like an opportunity. It is not necessary for him to be in the market continuously. He chooses only the best of what the tape offers.

His original risks can be gradually effaced by clever arrangement of stop orders when a stock goes his way. He may keep these in his head or put them on the "floor." For my own part I prefer, having decided upon a danger point, to maintain a mental stop and when the price is reached close the trade "at the market." Reason: There may be ground for a change of plan or opinion at the last moment; if a stop is on the floor it takes time to cancel or change it, hence there is a period of a few minutes when the operator does not know where he stands. By using mental stops and market orders he always knows where he stands, except as regards the prices at which his orders are executed. The main consideration is, he knows whether he is in or out.

The placing of stops is most effectual and scientific when indicated by the market itself. An example of this is as follows:

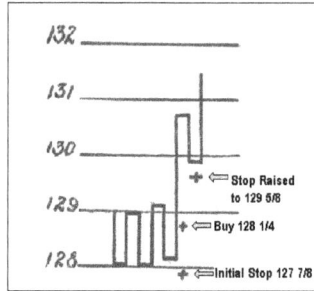

Here a stock, fluctuating between 128 and 129, gives a buying indication at 128 3/4.

Obviously, if the indication is true, the price will not again break 128, having met buying sufficiently strong to turn it up twice from that figure and a third time from 128 1/8. The fact that it did not touch 128 on the last down swing forecasts a higher up swing; it shows that the downward pressure was not so strong and the demand slightly larger and more urgent. In other words, the point of resistance was raised 1/8. Having bought at 128 3/4, the stop is placed at 127 7/8, which is ¼ below the last point of resistance. The stock goes above its previous top (129 1/8) and continues to 130 3/4. At any time after it has crossed 130 the trader may raise his stop to cost plus commission (129). The stock reacts at 129 7/8, then continues the advance to above 131. As soon as a new high point is reached the stop is raised to 129 5/8, as

129 7/8 was the point of resistance on the dip. In such a case the initial risk was 7/8 of a point plus commissions, etc...the market giving a well defined stop point, making an arbitrary stop not only unnecessary but expensive.

The illustration is given in chart form, but the experienced Tape Reader generally carries these swings in his head. A series of higher tops and bottoms are made in a pronounced up swing and the reverse in a down swing. Arbitrary stops may, of course, be used at any time, especially if one wishes to clinch a substantial profit, but until a stock gets away from the price at which it was entered, it seems best to use the stops it develops for itself.

If the operator is shaken out of his trade immediately after entering the trade, it does not prove his judgment was wrong. Some accident may have happened, some untoward development in a particular issue, of sufficient weight to affect the rest of the list. It is these unknown occurrences that make the limitation of losses most important. In such a case it would he folly to change the stop so that the risk is increased. This, while customary with the general invest-ing public, is something a professional Tape Reader seldom does. Each trade is made on its own basis, and for certain definite reasons. At the outset the amount of risk should be decided upon, and, except in very rare instances, should not he changed, except on the side of profit. The Tape Reader must eliminate, not increase, his risk. Averaging does not come within the province of the Tape Reader. Averaging is groping for the top or bottom. The Tape Reader must not grope. He must see and know, or he should not act.

It is impossible to fix a rule governing the amount of profit the operator should accept. In a general way, there should be no limit set as to the profits. A deal, when entered, may look as though it would yield three or four points, but if the strength increases with the advance it may run ten points before there is any sign of halt. We wish our readers to bear fully in mind that these recommendations and suggestions are not to be considered final or inflexible. It is not our aim to assume the role of an oracle. Rather, we are reasoning things out on paper, and as we progress in these studies and apply these tentative rules to the tape, in actual or paper trading, you probably have occasion to modify some of our conclusions.

A Tape Reader must close a trade: 1) when the tape tells him to close; 2) when his stop is caught; 3) when his position is not clear; 4) when he has a large or satisfactory profit and wishes to utilize those funds for better opportunities.

The first and most important reason for closing a trade is: The tape says so. This indication may appear in various forms. Assuming that one is trading in a Leader stock, the warning may come in the stock itself.

Within the recording of sales, there runs the fine silken thread of the trend. It is clearly distinguishable to one sufficiently versed in the art of Tape Reading, and, for reasons previously explained, is most readily observed in the leaders. So, when one is short of Union Pacific and this thread suddenly indicates that the market has turned upward, it's foolish to remain short. Not only must one cover quickly, but if the power of the movement is sufficient to warrant the risk, the operator must go long. In a market of sufficient breadth and swing, the Tape Reader will find that when it is time to close a trade, it is usually time to reverse his position. One must have the flexibility of whalebone, and entertain no rigid opinion. He must obey the tape implicitly. The indication to close a trade may come from another stock, several stocks or the general market.

For example, on the day of the Supreme Court decision in Consolidated Gas, suppose the operator was long of Union Pacific at 11 o'clock, having paid therefore 182 3/4. Between 11 and 12 o'clock Union rallied to 183 1/2, and Reading, which was more active, to 144. Just before, and immediately after, the noon hour, tremendous transactions took place in Reading, over 50,000 shares changing hands within three-quarters of a point. These may have been largely wash sales, accompanied by inside selling; it is impossible to tell. If they were not, the inference is that considerable buying power developed in Reading at this level and was met by selling heavy enough to supply all bidders and prevent the stock advancing above 144 3/8.

Large quantities coming within a small range indicated either one of two things: 1) That considerable buying power suddenly developed at this point, and the insiders chose to check it or to take advantage of the opportunity to unload. 2) The demonstration in Reading may have been intended to distract attention from other stocks in which large operators were unloading (there was no special evidence of this, except in New York Central). If the selling was not sufficient to check the upward move, the market for Reading would have absorbed all that was offered and advance to a higher level, but in this case the selling was more effectual than the buying, and Reading fell back, warning the operator that the temporary leader on the bull side of the market had met with defeat. At this point the operator was, therefore, on the lookout for a slump. Reading subsided, in small lots, back to 143 7/8. Union Pacific, after selling at 183 5/8, declined to 183 ¼. Both stocks developed dullness, and the whole market became more or less inactive.

Suddenly Union Pacific fell to 183 1/8. Then UP traded 500 shares @183, 200 at 182 7/8, 500 at 183, 200 at 182 7/8, and 500 at 182 3/4, indicating not only a lack of demand, but remarkably poor support. Immediately following this, New York Central, which sold only a few minutes before 400 shares at 131½ came 131 on 1700 shares, 130¼ on 500 shares and ended at 130 on 700 shares. This demonstrated that the market was remarkably hollow and in a position to develop great weakness. The large quantities of New York Central at the low figure, after a running decline of a point and one-half, showed that there was not only an absence of supporting orders, but that sellers were obliged to make great concessions in order to dispose of their holdings. The quantities, especially in view of the narrowness of the market, proved that the sellers were not small traders. Coupled with the wet blanket put on Reading and the poor support in Union Pacific, this weakness in New York Central was another advance notice of a decline.

On any indication of this kind, the trader must be ready to jump out of his long stock and get short of the market.

While waiting for his cue, the Tape Reader has time to consider which stock among the leaders is the most desirable
for selling. He quickly chooses Reading, on the ground that
the large lots which have apparently been distributed around
144 will probably come into the market as soon as weakness
develops. Reason: The general investing public generally
buys on just such peaks as the one which has taken place
in Reading. A large volume, even if accompanied by only
a fractional advance, has the effect of making the ordinary
trader intensely bullish, the result being that he bites off a
lot of long stock at the top of the market. This is exactly what
the manipulator wishes him to do. We have all heard people
boast that their purchase was at the top eighth and that it had
the effect of turning the stock down. Those who make their
purchases after this fashion are quickest to become scared
at the first sign of weakness, and throw overboard what they
have bought. First greed and then fear controlled them. In
choosing Reading, therefore, the Tape Reader is picking out
the stock in which he is likely to have the most help on the
bear side.

At 12.30 PM the market is standing still, the majority
of transactions being in small lots and then only fractional
changes. Reading shows the effect of the recent unloading.
It is coming out 500 at 143 3/4, 500 at 143 5/8, 400 at 143
½ and 400 at 143 3/4. The operator realizes that Reading is
probably a short sale right here, with a stop order at 144 1/2
or 5/8, on the ground that the bulls must have an extraordinary amount of buying power to push the stock above its
former top, where, at every eighth advance over 144 3/8,

they will encounter a considerable portion of 50,000 shares.

This reasoning, however, is all aside from our main argument, which is to show how the clue to get out of the stock will be given by the action of stocks other than that in which the trader is working. Union Pacific shows on the tape in small lots at 182 3/4; New York Central 1100 at 130, and 900 at 130 3/8. The rest of the market seems to have all the snap and ginger taken out of it and the operator does not like his position on the long side. He has no definite indication to sell short, however, he feels that his chances on the long side have been reduced to practically nothing by the weak undertone of the market, he therefore gets out of his Union Pacific and waits until the tape tells him to sell Reading short. Union Pacific weakens to182 5/8. The others slide off fractionally. The weakness is not strong enough to forecast any big break, so he continues to wait. There are 1800 shares of Union altogether at 182 5/8, followed by 3000 at 182 1/2. Other stocks respond and the market looks more bearish. Consolidated Gas trades 163¾ - 163 ¼ - 163. This is the first sign of activity in the stock, but the move is nothing unusual for Gas, as its fluctuations are generally wide and erratic. The balance of the list rallies a fraction. Gas trades 162 ½ to ¾, then 500 at 162 1/4. At this point Gas, which has been very dull up to now, forces itself, by its decline and weakness, upon the notice of the operator. He begins to look upon the stock as the possible shears which will cut the thread of the market and let everything down.

12.45 PM Gas trades 500 at 161 1/2. It is very weak. The balance of the list is steady, Union Pacific 182 5/8, Central

130 3/8, Reading 143 3/4. There is a fractional rally - Union Pacific to 182 7/8 and Gas to 162. Plenty of Central for sale around 130; Reading is 143 1/2. The rally peters out gradual weakening all around, but the Tape Reader cannot go with the trend until he is sure of a big move. Central trades at 129¾, showing that after all the buyers at 130 are filled up considerable stock is still for sale. The others show only in small lots. The market is on the verge of a decline; it is where a jar of any sort will start it down. Union Pacific is heavy at 182 1/2 - trades 300 at 182 3/8, 200 at 1/2; Reading 143 1/2, 3/8, and 1000 shares at 1/2; Central trades 2000 at 130 and 800 at 1/8.

Here is the thrust he has been looking for! Gas 163¾ on 200, 1/2 on 400, 161 on 300, 160 on 400! He waits no longer and gives an order to sell Reading short at the market. They are all on the run now, Reading 143 1/2, 600 at ¼, 1300 at 1/4. Central 130, 129 1/2, Gas trades 500 at 159 1/2. Something's very rotten about Gas and it's a cinch to sell it short if you don't mind trading in a buzz-saw stock. The market breaks so rapidly that he does not get over 142 3/4 for his Reading, but he is short not far from the top of what looks like a wide open break. Everything is slumping now - Steel, Smelters, Southern Pacific, St. Paul. Union Pacific is down to 181 5/8 and the rest in proportion. Gas 158 1/2,158 on 300, 157, 156, 155, 154, 153 and the rest "come tumbling after." Reading 141 3/8, 500 at ¼, 400 at 141, 140 3/4, 500 at 1/2, 200 at 140, 600 at 139 3/4, 500 at 5/8. Union 181 - 180 7/8, 3/4, 1/2, 1/4, 600 at 1/8, 500 at 180, 179 3/4, 500 at 1/2, 300 at 1/4, Central 127 1/2.

The above illustrates some of the workings of a Tape Reader's mind; also how a break in a stock, entirely foreign to that which is being traded in, will furnish an indication to get out and go short of one stock or another. The indication to close a trade may come from the general market where the trend is clearly developed throughout the list all stocks working in complete harmony. One of the best indications in this line is the strength or weakness on rallies and reactions.

Of course the break in Gas, which finally touched 138, was due to the Supreme Court decision, announced on the news tickers at 1:10 PM, but, as is usually the case, the tape told the news many minutes before anything else. This is one of the advantages of getting your news from the first place where it is reflected. Other people who wait for such information to sift through telephone wires and reach them by the round-about way of news tickers or word of mouth, are working under a tremendous handicap. That not even the insiders knew what the decision was to be - is shown in the dullness of the stock all morning. Those who heard the decision in the Supreme Court chamber doubtless went straight to the telephone and sold the stock short. Their sales showed on the tape before the news arrived in New York. Tape Readers were, therefore, first to be notified. They were short before the Street knew what had happened.

CHAPTER FIVE
Volumes and Their Significance

AS the whole object of these studies is to learn to read what the tape says, I will now explain a point which should be known and understood before we proceed, otherwise the explanations cannot be made clear.

First of all, we must recognize that the market for any stock - at whatever level it may be - is composed of two sides, represented by the bid and the asking price. Remember that the "last sale" is something entirely different from the "market price." If Steel has just sold at 50, this figure represents what has happened. It's history. The market price of Steel is either 49 1/8@50 or 50@50 1/8. The bid and asked prices combined form the market price. This market price is like a pair of scales, and the volume of stock thrown out by sellers and reached for by purchasers, shows toward which side the preponderance of weight has momentarily shifted. For example, when the tape shows the market price is 50 1/8, and the large volumes are on the up side.

US

500 @ 50

1000 @ 50 1/8

200 @ 50

1500 @ 50 1/8

In these four transactions there are 700 shares sold at 50 versus 2500 bought at 50 1/8, proving that at the moment the buying is more effective than the selling. The deduction to be made from this is that Steel will probably sell at 50 1/4 before 49 7/8. There is no certainty, because supply and demand is changing with every second, not only in Steel but in every other stock on the list.

Here is one advantage in trading only the leaders: The influence of demand or pressure is first evidenced in the principal stocks. The hand of the dominant power, whether it be an insider, an outside manipulator or the public, is shown in these volumes. The reason is simple. The big fellows cannot put their stocks up or down without trading in large amounts. In an advancing market they are obliged to reach up for or bid up their stocks, as, for example:

US

1000 @ 182 1/8

200 @182

1500 @ 182 1/8

200 @ 182 1/4

3500 @ 182 3/8

2000 @ 182 1/2

Take some opening trades and subsequent transactions like the following:

200... 47 1/4

100... 45 7/8

100... 45 7/8

1900... 46 3/4

100... 46 1/8

100... 46

100... 46 5/8

100... 46

600... 45 7/8

100... 46 1/2

200... 46 1/4

500... 45 3/4

100... 46 3/8

100... 46 3/8

200... 45 5/8

600... 46 1/4

11 A. M.

100... 45 1/2

100... 46 1/8

300... 46 3/8

100... 45 5/8

600... 46

100... 46 1/8

400... 45 7/8

100... 45 7/8

100... 46

100... 45 3/4

200... 45 3/4

100... 45 7/8

400... 45 5/8

100... 46

100... 46

100... 45 3/4

Here the opening market price was 46 3/4 bid @ 47¼ asking, and the buyers of 200 shares "at the market" paid the high price. All bids at 46 3/4 were then filled. This is proved by the next sale, which is at 46 5/8. The big lots thereafter are mostly on the down side, showing that pressure still existed. The indications were, therefore, that the stock would go lower. A lot of 1900 shares in some stocks would be a large quantity; in others insignificant. These points have a relative value with which traders must familiarize themselves. Volumes must be considered in proportion to the activity of the market, as well as the relative activity of that particular issue . No set rule can be established. I have seen a Tape Reader make money by following the lead of a looo share lot of Northwest which someone took at a fraction above the last sale. Ordinarily Northwest is a sluggish investment stock, and this size lot appeared as the fore-runner of an active speculative demand.

Now let us see what happens on the floor to produce the above-described effect on the tape. Let's prove that our method is correct.

A few years ago the control of a certain railroad was being bought on the floor of the New York Stock Exchange. One brokerage house was given all the orders, with instructions to distribute them and conceal the buying as much as possible. The original order for the day would read, "Take everything that is offered up to 38".

38 was about 3 points above the market of the day before. This left considerable leeway for the broker to whom the buying order was entrusted. He would instruct his floor broker as follows: "The stock closed last night at 35. You take everything offered up to 35 1/2 and then report to me how things stand. Don't bid for the stock - just take it as it is offered and mark it down whenever you can". In such a case the floor member stands in the crowd awaiting the opening. On the markets open the chairman's gavel strikes and the crowd begins yelling. Someone offers "Two Thousand at an eighth." Another broker says "Thirty-five for five hundred." Our broker takes the 2000 at an 1/8 then offers one hundred at one-eighth himself, so as to keep the price down. Others also offer one or two hundred shares at 1/8, so he withdraws his offer, as he wishes to accumulate and only offers or sells when it helps him buy more, or puts the price down.

The buyer at 35 has 300 shares of his lot cancelled, so he alters his bid to "thirty- five for two hundred." The other sellers supply him and he then bids "7/8 for a hundred." Our broker sells him 100 at 7/8 just to get the price down. Someone comes in with "a thousand at five." Our broker says, "I'll take it." Five hundred more is offered at 1/8. This he also takes.

Let us see how the tape records these transactions:

Open 35

2000 @ 35 1/8

200 @ 35

100 @ 34 /7/8

100 @ 35

500 @ 35 1/8

The day trader interprets these transactions: Opening bid and asked price was 35 1/8 someone took the large lot (2000 shares) at the high price. The two sales following were in small lots, showing light pressure. The 100 @ 35 after 34 7/8 shows that on the "7/8 bid" -"5 ask" market the buyer took the stock at the offered price and followed it up by taking 500 more at the eighth. The demand is dominant and it does not matter whether the buyer is one individual or a dozen, the momentary trend is upward.

To get the opposite side, let us suppose that a manipulator is desirous of depressing a stock. This can be accomplished by offering and selling more than there is a demand for, or by coaxing or frightening other holders into throwing over their shares. It makes no difference whose stock is sold;

"The Lord is on the side of the heaviest battalions," as men used to say. When a manipulator puts a broker into a crowd with orders to mark it down, the broker supplies all bids and then offers it down to the objective point or until he meets resistance too strong for him to overcome without the loss of a large block of stock.

The stock in question is selling around 80, we will say, and the broker's orders are to "put it to 77." Going into the crowd, he finds 500 wanted at 79 7/8 and 300 offered at 80. Last sale, 100 at 80. "I'll sell you that five hundred at seven-eighths. A thousand or any part at three quarters," he shouts. "I'll take two hundred at three-quarters," says another broker. "A half for five hundred," is heard. "Sold!" is the response. "A half for five hundred more." "Sold 1" "That's a thousand I sold you at a half. Five hundred at three-eighths!" "I'll take a hundred at three-eighths," comes a voice. "You're on!" is the reply. "Quarter for five hundred." "Sold!" is the quick response.

His pounding of the stock would reveal itself on the tape as follows:

Open 80

500 sold@ 79 7/8

200 sold@ 79 3/4

1000 sold@ 79 ½

500 sold @79 ¼

If he met strong resistance at 79 it would appear on the tape something like this:

1000 sold @ 79

500 sold @ 79

800 @ 79

300 @ 79 1/8

1000 @ 79

500 @ 79 1/4

200 @ 79 1/2

...showing that at 79 there was a demand for more than he was willing to supply. (For example: There might have been 10,000 shares still wanted at 79 which is more than he could supply). Frequently a broker meeting such an obstacle will leave the crowd long enough to phone his principal. His departure opens the way for a rally, as the stock is no longer under pressure, and the large buying order at 79 acts as a back log for floor traders. So those in the crowd bid it up to

79 1/2 in hopes of scalping a fraction on the long side.

Take another case where two brokers are put into the crowd - one to depress the stock and the other to accumulate it. They play into each other's hands, and the tape makes the following report of what happens:

Open 80 1/8 - 80

200 @ 79 7/8

1000 @ 79 7/8

200 @ 79 5/8

500 @ 79 3/4

300 @ 79 3/4

1500 @ 79 1/2

500 @ 79 1/4

100 @ 79 1/8

Were we on the floor we should see one broker offering the stock down, while the other grabbed every round lot that appeared. We cannot tell how far down the stock will be put, but when these indications appear it makes us watch closely for the turning point, which is our time to buy. The Tape Reader does not care whether a move is made by a manipulator, a group of floor traders, the public or a combination of all. The figures on the tape represent the consensus of opinion, the effect of manipulation and the supply and demand, all combined. That is why tape indications are more reliable than what anyone hears, knows or thinks.

With the illustration of the pair of scales (supply – demand) clearly implanted in our minds, we scan the moment by moment transactions of the tape, mentally weighing each indication in our effort to learn on which side the tendency is strongest. Not a detail must escape our notice. A sudden demand or a burst of liquidation may enable us to form a new plan, revise an old one or prompt us to assume a neutral attitude.

These volume indications are not always clear. Nor are they infallible. It doesn't do any good to rely upon the indications of any one stock to the exclusion of the rest. There are times when certain stocks are run up, while volume indications in other active stocks show clearly that they are being distributed as fast as the market will take them. This happens frequently on a large or small scale. Especially is it apparent at the turning point of a big swing, where accumulation or distribution requires several days to complete.

Volumes can be studied from the reports printed in the Wall Street Journal, but the real way to study them is from the tape. If you are not able to spend five to seven hours a day at the tape while the ticker is in operation, you can arrange to have the tape saved for you each day. The tape can then be studied at leisure. In studying under these conditions let it be on as small a scale as you like, but make actual trades with real money.

There are times when the foregoing rule of volumes indicates almost the reverse of what we have explained. One of these instances was described in our last chapter. In this case the transactions in Reading suddenly swelled out of all proportion to the rest of the market and its own previous volume.

700... 143 5/8

500... 143 3/4

5000... 143 5/8

1700... 143 3/4

200... 143 5/8

4300... 143 3/4

3700... 143 7/8

100... 144

12 P.M.

5000... 144

1300... 143 7/8

3000... 144

5000... 144 1/8

2100... 144 1/4

2200... 144 1/8

3500... 144 1/4

4000... 144 3/8

3000... 144 1/4

2500... 144 1/8

3500... 144

400... 144 1/8

1000... 144

500.... 144 1/8

1100... 144

2000... 143 7/8

2500... 143 3/4

1000... 143 5/8

Notwithstanding the predominance of apparent demand, the resistance offered (whether legitimate or artificial) became too great for the stock to overcome, and it fell back from 144 3/8. On the way up these volumes suggested a purchase, but the tape showed abnormal transactions, accompanied by poor response from the rest of the list. This smacked of manipulation and warned the operator to be cautious on the bull side. The large volume in Reading was sustained even after the stock reacted, but the large lots were evidently thrown over at the bid prices. On the way up the volumes were nearly all on the up side and the small lots on the down side. After 144 3/8 was reached the large lots were on the down side and the small lots on the up.

It is just as important to study the small lots as the large lots. The smaller quantities are like the feathers on an arrow - they indicate that the business part of the arrow is at the other end. In other words, the smaller lots keep one constantly informed as to what fraction forms the other side of the market. For example: During the first five trades in Reading, recorded above, the market quotation is shown to have been 5/8@3/4; it then changed to 3/4@7/8 and again to 7/8@4. On the way down it got to be 4@1/8, and at this level the small lots were particularly valuable in showing the pressure that existed.

Stocks like Union, Reading and Steel usually make this sort of a turning point on a volume of from 25,000 to 50,000 shares. That is, when they meet with opposition on an advance or a decline it must be in some such quantity in order to stem the tide. Walk into the hilly country and you will find a small river running quietly on its way. The stream is so tiny that you can place your hand in its course and the water will back up. In five minutes, it overcomes this resistance by going over or around your hand. You fetch a shovel, pile dirt in its path, pack it down hard and say, "There, I've dammed you up".

But you haven't at all, for the next day you find your pile of dirt washed away. You bring cartloads of dirt and build a substantial dam, and the flow is finally held in check. It is the same with an individual stocks or the market. Prices follow the line of least resistance. If Reading is going up someone may throw 10,000 shares in its path without perceptible effect. Another lot of 20,000 shares follows; the stock halts, but finally overcomes the obstacle. The seller gives another order - this time 30,000 shares more are thrown on the market. If there are 30,100 shares wanted at that level, the buyer will absorb all of the 30,000 and the stock will go higher; if only 29,900 shares are needed to fill all bids, the price will recede because demand has been overcome by supply.

It looks as though something like this happened in Reading on the occasion referred to. Whether or not manipulative orders predominated does not change the aspect of the case. In the final test the weight was on the down side.

The public and the floor traders do not stand aside while the manipulator is at work, nor is the reverse true. Everybody's stock looks alike on the tape.

When a stream breaks through a dam it goes into new territory. Likewise the breaking through of a stock is significant, because it means that the resistance has been overcome. The stronger the resistance, the less likelihood of finding further obstacles in the immediate vicinity. Dams are not usually built one behind the other. So when we find a stock emerging into a new field it is best to go with it, especially if, in breaking through it, it carries the rest of the market along.

While a lot can be learned from the reports printed in the daily newspapers mentioned above, the moment by moment transactions – trades as they appear - is the only real instruction book. A live tape is to be preferred, for the element of speed with which you receive the information is of no small concern. The comparative activity of the market on peaks and breaks is a guide to the technical condition of the market. For instance, during a decline, if the ticker is very active and the volume of sales large, voluntary or compulsory liquidation is indicated. This is emphasized if, on the subsequent rally, the tape moves sluggishly and only small lots appear. In an active bull market the ticker appears to be choked with the volume of sales poured through it on the advances, but on reactions the quantities and the number of impressions decrease until, like tile ocean at ebb tide, the market is almost lifeless.

Another indication of the power of a movement is found in the differences between sales of active stocks, for example:

1000 @ 180

100 @ 180 1/8

500 @ 180 3/8

1000 @ 180 1/2

This shows that there was only 100 shares for sale at 180 1/8, none at all at 180¼, and only 500 at 3/8. The jump from 1/8 to 3/8 emphasizes both the absence of pressure and persistency on the part of the buyers. They are not content to wait patiently until they can secure the stock at 180¼; they "reach" for it. On the opposite side this would show lack of support.

Each indication is to be judged not so much by rule as according to the conditions surrounding it. The tape furnishes a continuous series of motion pictures, with their respective explanations written between the printings. These motion pictures of the market are in a language which is foreign to all casual investors – but understandable to the professional Tape Reader.

A number of people who have read previous editions of this book have been misled by the apparent ease with which some kinds of markets may be read by means of the volumes. They have erroneously come to the conclusion that all one has to do is sit beside a ticker and observe which side the volumes are on - the buying or the selling side. This is a mistake. Under the old exchange rule a buyer who desired to influence the market in an upward direction could bid for 10,000 shares or any other very large quantity, and no one could sell him any less than the quantity bid for, unless the buyer was willing to take it. Under the present rules, the buyer is obliged to take any part of 10,000 shares, or whatever quantity he bid for if he does not specify "all or none" to his broker. This revision of the rules, and the other restrictions against matched orders, manipulations, etc., eliminates a very large number of transactions in big quantities at the advanced or the decreased price. It was an old trick of Harriman's and some of the old Standard Oil party, as well as other minor manipulators and floor traders, to make these bids and offers in round lots and have some one else supply or take them for its effect on the market. But the change in the rules has greatly reduced the volume and decreased the value of these indications. Hence, while they are still very suggestive to an observant tape reader, and while the principle is unchanged, it will not do to depend on them entirely.

The volumes which we have been discussing are least liable to mislead when manipulation prevails, for the manipulator is obliged to deal in large blocks of stock, and must continually show his hand. A complete manipulative operation on the long side consists of three parts: 1) Accumulation, 2) marking up, and 3) distribution. In the case of a shorting operation - the distribution comes first, then the mark down and the accumulation.

No one of these three sections is complete without the other two. The manipulator must work with a large block of stock or the deal will not be worth his time, the risk and expenses. The Tape Reader must therefore, be on the lookout for extensive operations on either side of the market. Accumulation will show itself in the quantities and in the way they appear on the tape. He does not buy it at once, because it may take weeks or months for the manipulator to complete the accumulation of his line, and there might be opportunities to buy cheaper. By holding off until the psychological moment he forces someone else to carry the stock for him - to pay his interest.

Furthermore, his capital is left free in the meantime. When the marking up begins he gets in at the commencement of the move, and goes along with it till there are signs of a halt or distribution. Having passed through the first two periods, he is in a position to fully benefit by the third stage of the operation. In this sort of work a figure chart, which I described in another chapter, will help the trader, especially if the manipulative operation is continued over a considerable period of time. It will give him a bird's-eye view of the deal, enabling him to drop or resume the thread at any stage.

CHAPTER SIX
Market Technique

ON Saturday morning, February 27, 1909, the market opened slightly higher than the previous night's close. Reading was the most active stock. After touching 123 1/2 it slid off to 122 1/2, at which point it invited short sales. This indication was emphasized at 122, at 121 1/2 and again at 121. The downward trend was strongly marked until it struck 119 7/8, then it followed a quick rally of 1 1/8 points.

This was a vicious three-point jab into a market that was only just recovering from a decline in early February. What was its effect on the other principal stocks? Union Pacific declined only 3/4, Southern Pacific 5/8 and Steel 5/8. This proved that they were technically strong; that is, they were in hands which could view with equanimity a three-point break in a leading issue. Had this drive occurred when Reading was around 145 and Union 185 the effect upon the others would probably have been very different.

In order to determine the extent of an ore body, miners use a diamond drill. This produces a core, the character of which shows what is beneath the surface. If it had been possible to have drilled into the market at the top of the foregoing rise, we should have found that the bulk of the floating supply in Steel, Reading and some others was held by a class of traders who buy heavily in booms and on bulges. These people operate with comparatively small margins, nerve and experience. They are exceedingly vulnerable, so the stocks in which they operate suffer the greatest declines when the market receives a jar.

The figures are interesting:

	1907-09 Advance	Feb 09 Decline	% Break to Advance
U.P.	84 1/4	12 3/8	14.7
Reading	73 1/4	26 3/8	33.6
Steel	36 1/4	16 1/2	44.6

The above shows that the public was heavily extended in Steel somewhat less loaded with Reading, and was carrying very little Union Pacific. In other words, Union showed technical strength by its resistance to pressure, whereas Reading and Steel offered little or no opposition to the decline.

Both the market as a whole and individual stocks are to be judged as much by what they do as what they do not do at critical points. If the big fellows who accumulated Union below 120 had distributed it above 180, the stock would have broken something like thirty points, due to its having passed from strong to weak hands. As it did not have any such decline, but only a very small reaction compared to its advance, the Tape Reader infers that Union is destined for much higher prices; that it offers comparative immunity from declines and a possible large advance in the near future.

Even were Union Pacific scheduled for a thirty-point rise in the following two weeks, something might happen to postpone the campaign for a considerable time. But the Tape Reader must work with these broader considerations in full view. He has just so much time and capital, and this must be employed where it will yield the greatest results. If by watching for the most favourable opportunities he can operate with the trend in a stock which will some day or week show him ten points profit more than any other issue he could have chosen, be is increasing his chances to that extent.

A long advance or decline usually culminates in a wide, quick movement in the leaders. Take the break of February 23, 1909: Reading declined from 128 3/4 to 118 and Steel from 46 to 41 1/4 in one day. Southern Pacific, after creeping up from 97 to 112, reached a climax in a seven-point jump during one session.

Instances are so numerous that they are hardly worth citing. The same thing happens in the market as a whole - an exceptionally violent movement, after a protracted sag or rise, usually indicates its termination. A stock generally shows the Tape Reader what it proposes to do by its action under pressure or stimulation. For example: On Friday, February 19, 1909, the United States Steel Corporation announced an open market in steel products. The news was out. Everybody in the country knew it by the following morning. The Tape Reader, in weighing the situation before the next day's opening, would reason – "As the news is public property, the normal thing for Steel and the market to do is to rally. Steel closed last night at 48 3/8. The market hinges upon this one stock. Let's see how it acts." The opening price of U. S. Steel was three-quarters of a point down from the previous closing - a perfectly natural occurrence in view of the announcement. The real test of strength or weakness will follow. For the first ten minutes

Steel shows on the tape:

200 @ 47 7/8
4500 @ 47 3/4
1200 @ 47 7/8
1500 @ 47 3/4

...without otherwise varying. Eighteen times the price swings back and forth between the same fractions.

Meanwhile, Union Pacific, which opened at 177 1/2, shows a tendency to rally and pull the rest of the market up behind it. Can Union lift Steel? That is the question. Here are two opposing forces, and the Tape Reader watches like a hawk, for he is "going with the market" - in the direction of the trend. Union is up 7/8 from the opening and Southern Pacific is reinforcing it. But Steel does not respond. Not once does it get out of that 3/4 - 7/8 rut - not even single hundred share lot can be sold at 48. This proves that it is freely offered at 47 7/8 and that it possesses no rallying power, in spite of the leadership displayed by the Harrimans.

Union seems to make a final effort to induce a following:

2000 @ 178 1/2

...to which Steel replies by breaking through with a thud:

800 @ 47 5/8

This is the Tape Reader's cue to go short. In an instant he has put out a line of Steel for which he gets 47 1/2 or 47 3/8 as there are large volumes traded in at those figures. Union Pacific seems disheartened. The Steel millstone is hanging round its neck. It slides off to 178 ¾, ¼, 1/8 and finally to 177 7/8.

The pressure on Steel increases at the low level. Successive sales are made as follows.

6800 @ 47 ½

2600 @ 47 3/8

500 @ 47 1/4

8800 @ 47 1/8

From this time on there is a steady flow of long stock all through the list. Reading and Pennsylvania are the weakest railroads. Colorado Fuel breaks seven points in a running decline and the other steel stocks follow suit. U.S. Steel is dumped in bunches at the bid prices, and even the dignified preferred is sympathetically affected.

At the end of the two hour session, the market closes at the bottom, with Steel at 46, leaving thousands of accounts weakened by the decline and a holiday ahead for holders to worry over. It looks to the Tape Reader as though the stock would go lower on the following Tuesday. At any rate, no covering indication has appeared, and unless it is his invariable rule to close every trade each day, he puts a stop at 47 on his short Steel and goes his way. (His original stop was

48 1/8). Steel opens on the following session at 44 ¾ @ 1/2, and during the day makes a low record of 41¼.

A number of lessons may be drawn from this episode. Successful tape reading is a study of force; it requires ability to judge which side has the greatest pulling power and one must have the courage to go with that side. There are critical points which occur in each swing, just as in the life of a business or of an individual. At these junctures it seems as though a feather's weight on either side would determine the immediate critical trend. Any one who can spot these points has much to win and little to lose, for he can always play with a stop placed close behind the turning point or "point of resistance".

If Union had continued in its upward course, gaining in power, volume and influence as it progressed, the dire effects of the Steel situation might have been overcome. It was simply a question of power, and Steel pulled Union down. This study of 'responses' to stimulation or outside influences on stocks is one of the most valuable in the Tape Reader's education. It is an almost unerring guide to the technical position of the market. Of course, all responses are not so clearly defined.

It is a matter of indifference to the Tape Reader as to who or what produces these tests, or critical periods. They constantly appear and disappear; he must make his diagnosis and act accordingly. If a stock is being manipulated higher, the movement will seldom be continued unless other stocks follow and support the advance. Barring certain specific developments affecting a stock, the other issues should be watched to see whether large operators are unloading on the strong spots. Should a stock fail to break on bad news, it means that insiders have anticipated the decline and stand ready to buy.

A member of a trading syndicate once said to me: "We are going to dissolve tomorrow." I asked, "Won't there be considerable selling by people who don't want to carry their share of the securities?" "Oh!" he replied, "we know how every one stands. Probably 10,000 shares will come on the market from a few members who are obliged to sell, and as a few of us have sold that much short in anticipation, we'll be there to buy it when the time comes." This reminds us that it is well to consider the insider's probable attitude on a stock.

The tape usually indicates what this is. One of the muckraking magazines once showed that Rock Island preferred had been driven down to 28 one August to the accompaniment of receivership rumours. The writer of the article was unable to prove that these rumours originated with the insiders, for he admitted that the transactions at the time were not fully understood. Perhaps they were inscrutable to a person inexperienced in tape reading, but we well remember that the indications were all in favour of buying the stock on the break. The transactions were very large - out of all proportion to the capital stock outstanding and the floating supply.

What did this mean to the Tape Reader? Thousands of shares of stock were traded in per day, after a ten-point decline and a small rally. If the volume of sales represented long stock, someone was there to buy it. If there was manipulation it certainly was not for the purpose of distributing the stock at such a low level.

So, by casting out the unlikely factors, a Tape Reader could have arrived at the correct conclusion. The market is being put to the test continually by one element of which little has been said, i.e., the floor traders. These shrewd fellows are always on the alert to ferret out a weak spot in the market, for they love the short side. Lack of support, if detected, in an issue generally leads to a raid which, if the technical situation is weak, spreads to other parts of the floor and produces a reaction or a slump all around. Or, if they find a vulnerable short interest, they are quick to bid up a stock and drive the shorts to cover.

With these and other operations going on all the time, the Tape Reader who is at all expert is seldom at a loss to know on which side his best chances lie. Other people are doing for him what he would do himself if he were all-powerful. While it is the smaller swings that interest him most, the day trader must not fail to keep his bearings in relation to the broader movements of the market. When a panic prevails he recognizes it in the birth of a bull market and operates with the certainty that prices will gradually rise until a boom marks the other extreme of the swing. In a bull market he considers reactions of from two to five points normal and reasonable.

He looks for occasional drops of 10 to 15 points in the leaders, with a 25-point break at least once a year. When any of these occur, he knows what to look for next. In a bull market he expects a drop of 10 points to be followed by a recovery of about half the decline, and if the rise is to continue, all of the drop and more will be recovered. If a stock or the market refuses to rally naturally, he knows that the trouble has not been overcome, and therefore looks for a further decline.

Take American Smelters, which made a top of 99 5/8 a few years ago, then slumped off under rumours of competition until it reached 78. Covering indications appeared around 79 1/2. Had the operator also gone long here, he could confidently have expected Smelters to rally to about 89. The decline having been 21 5/8 points, there was a rally of 10 3/4 points due. As a matter of record the stock did recover to 89 3/8.

Of course, these things are mere guide posts, as the Tape Reader's actual trading is done only on the most positive and promising indications; but they are valuable in teaching him what to avoid. For instance, he would be wary about making an initial short sale of Smelters after a 15 point break, even if his indications were clear. There might be several points more on the short side, but he would realize that every point further decline would bring him closer to the turning point, and after such a violent break the safest money was to wait for an opportunity on the long side. Another instance: Reading sold on January 4, 1909, at 144 3/8. By the end of the month it touched 1311/2, and on February 23rd broke ten points to 118. This was a decline of 24 3/8 points (allowing for the 2 per cent dividend paid). As previously stated, the stock looked like an attractive short sale, not only on the first breakdown, but on the final drive. The conservative trader would have waited for a buying indication, as there would have been less risk on the long side.

It is seldom that the market runs more than three or four consecutive days in one direction without a reaction, so the Tape Reader must realize that his chances decrease as the swing is prolonged. The daily movements offer his best opportunities; but he must keep in stocks which swing wide enough to enable him to secure a profit. As Napoleon said: "The adroit man profits by everything, neglects nothing which may increase his chances".

I once knew a speculator who bought and sold by the clock. He had no idea of the hourly swing, but would buy at 12 o'clock, because it was 12 o'clock, and would sell at 2 o'clock, for the same reason. The methods employed by the average outside speculator are not so very much of an improvement on this, and that is why so many lose their money. The expert Tape Reader is diametrically opposed to such people and their methods. He applies science and skill in angling for profits. He studies, figures, analyzes and deduces. He knows exactly where he stands, what he is doing and why.

CHAPTER SEVEN
Dull Markets and their Opportunities

MANY people are apt to regard a dull market as a problem for trading purposes. They claim: "Our hands are tied; we can't get out of what we've got; if we could there'd be no use getting in again, for whatever we do we can't make a dollar".

Such people are not Tape Readers. They are Sitters. As a matter of fact, dull markets offer innumerable opportunities and we have only to dig beneath the crust of prejudice to find them.

Dullness in the market or in any special stock means that the forces capable of influencing it in either an upward or a downward direction have temporarily come to a balance. The best illustration is that of a clock which is about run down - its pendulum gradually decreases the width of its swings until it comes to a complete standstill, like this:

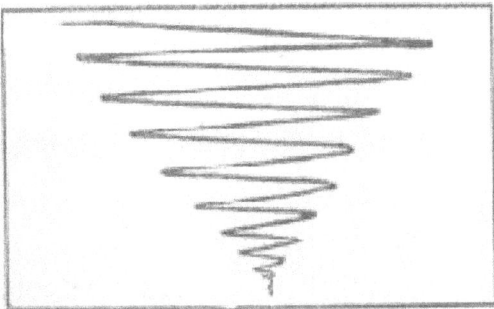

How the market pendulum comes to a standstill

Turn this diagram sideways and you see what the chart of a stock or the market looks like when it reaches the point of dullness:

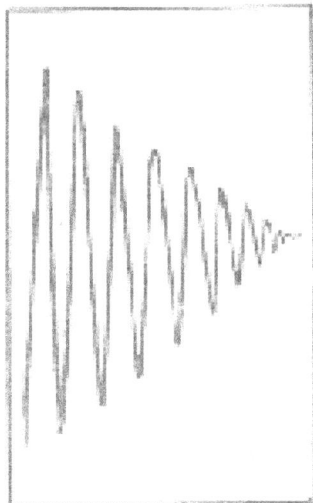

These dull periods often occur after a season of delirious activity on the bull side. People make money, pyramid on their profits and glut themselves with stocks at the top. As every one is loaded up, there is comparatively no one left to buy, and the break which inevitably follows would happen if there were no bears, no bad news or anything else to force a decline.

Nature has her own remedy for dissipation. She presents the debauch with its start, its climax and its collapse, with a thumping head and a moquette tongue. These tend to keep him quiet until the damage can be repaired. So with these intervals of market rest. Traders who have placed themselves in a position to be trimmed are duly trimmed. They lose their money and temporarily, their nerve. The market, therefore, becomes neglected. Extreme dullness sets in.

If the history of the market were to be written, these periods of lifelessness should mark the close of each chapter. The reason is: The factors that were active in producing the main movement, with its start, its climax and its collapse, have spent their force. Prices, therefore, settle into a groove, where they remain sometimes for weeks or until affected by some other powerful influence.

When a market is in the midst of a big move, no one can tell how long or how far it will run. But when prices are stationary, we know that from this point there will be a pronounced swing in one direction or another. There are ways of anticipating the direction of this swing. One is by noting the technical strength or weakness of the market, as described in a previous chapter. The resistance to pressure mentioned as characteristic of the dull period in March, 1909, was followed by a pronounced rise, leading stocks selling many points higher.

This was particularly true of Reading, in which the shake-outs around 120 (one of which was described) were frequent and positive. When insiders shake other people out it means that they want the stock themselves. These are good times for us to get in. When a dull market shows its inability to hold rallies, or when it does not respond to bullish news, it is technically weak, and unless something comes along to change the situation, the next swing will be downward. On the other hand, when there is a gradual hardening in prices; when bear raids fail to dislodge considerable quantities of stock; when stocks do not decline upon unfavourable news, we may look for an advancing market in the near future.

No one can tell when a dull market will merge into a very active one, therefore the Tape Reader must be constantly on the watch. It is foolish for him to say: "The market is dead dull. No use watching it today. The leaders only swung less than a point yesterday. Nothing profitable can happen in such a market". Such reasoning is apt to make one miss the very choicest opportunities - those of getting in on the ground floor of a big move.

For example: During the previous mentioned accumulation in Reading, the stock ranged between 120 and 124 1/2. Without warning, it one day gave indication (around 125) that the absorption was about concluded, and the stock had begun its advance. The Tape Reader having reasoned beforehand that this accumulation was no small investors game, would have grabbed a bunch of Reading as soon as the indication appeared. He might have bought more than he wanted for scalping purposes, with the intention of holding part of his line for a long swing, using the rest for regular trading. As the stock drew away from his purchase price he could have raised his stop on the lot he intended to hold, putting a mental label on it to the effect that it is to be sold when he detects inside distribution.

Thus he stands to benefit to the fullest extent by any manipulative work which may be done. In other words, he says: "I'll get out of this lot when the big boys and their friends get out of theirs". He feels easy in his mind about this stock, because he has seen the accumulation and knows it has relieved the market of all the floating supply at about this level. This means a sharp, quick rise sooner or later, as little stock is to be met with on the way up.

If he neglected to watch the market continuously and get in at the very start, his chances would be greatly lessened. He might not have the courage to take on the larger quantity. On Friday, March 26, 1909. Reading and Union were about as dull as two gentlemanly leaders could well be. Reading opened at 132 3/4, high was 133¼, low 132¼, last 132 5/8. Union's extreme fluctuation was 5/8! - from 180 5/8 to 181¼. Activity was confined to Beet Sugar, Kansas City Southern, etc.

The following day, Saturday, the opening gave every indication that the previous day's dullness would be repeated, initial sales showing only fractional changes. Let's see... B. & o., Wabash pfd. and Missouri Pacific were up 3/8 or 1/2. Union was an 1/8th higher and Reading 1/8 lower. Beet Sugar was down 5/8, with sales at 32. Reading showed 1100 @ 132¼, 800 @ 3/8, Union 800 @ 181, 400 @ 181, 200 @ 181 1/8, 400 @ 181. A single hundred Steel at 45½ 1/8. B& O 100 @ 109 7/8.

Market dead, mostly single 100 share lots... Ah! Here's our cue! Reading 2300 @ 132½., 2000 @ ½, 500 @ 5/8. Coming out of a dead market, quantities like these taken at the offered prices can mean only one thing, and without argument the Tape Reader takes on a bunch of Reading "at the market." Whatever is happening in Reading, the rest of the market is slow to respond, although N. Y. Central seems willing to help a little – 500 @ 127½ (after ¼). Beets are up to 33¼. Steel is 45 1/8, and Copper 77 ¼ -a fraction better. Reading 300 @ 132/2. Steel 1300 @ 45 1/8, ¼ Union 100 @ 181 Reading 300 @ 132 5/8 Beets 100 @ 33½. Union 700 @ 181½ N.Y. Central 127 5/8, 600 @ ¾... 7/8!...There's some help coming! Union 900 @ 181½ now Reading 100 @ 132 3/4. Copper 700 @ 71½. Reading 800 @ 132 7/8, 100 @ 133, 900 @ 133, 1100 @ 1/8... Reading 1500 @ 133¼ , 3500 @ 133 ½...not much doubt about the trend now.

The whole market is responding to Reading, and there is a steady increase in power, breadth and volume. The rapid advances show that short covering is no small factor. It looks as though a lot of people are throwing their Beet Sugar and getting into the big stocks. St. Paul Copper and Smelters begin to lift a little. Around 11 A.M. there is a brief period of hesitation, in which the market seems to take a long breath in preparation for another effort. There is scarcely any reaction and no weakness. Reading backs up a fraction to 133¼ and Union to 181 3/8.

There are no selling indications, so the Tape Reader stands by his guns. Now they are picking up again... Reading 133 3/8, ½, 5/8, ¾... Union 181 5/8 N.Y. Central 128½ 1/8, 700 @ ¼, Union 1000 @ 181½, 3500 @ 5/8, 2800 @ 7/8, 4100 @ 182 Steel 45 ½.... From then right up to the close it's nothing but bull, and everything closes within a fraction of its highest. Reading makes 134 3/8, Union 183, Steel 46 1/8, Central 128 7/8, and the rest in proportion. The market has gained such headway that it will take dire news to prevent a high, wide opening on Monday, and the Tape Reader has his choice of closing out at the high point or putting in a stop and taking his chances over Sunday.

So we see the advantage of watching a dull market and getting in the moment it starts out of its rut. One could almost draw lines on the chart of a leader like Union or Reading (the upper line being the high point of its monotonous swing and the lower line the low point) and buy or sell whenever the line is crossed. Because when a stock shakes itself loose from a narrow radius it is clear that the accumulation or distribution or resting spell has been completed and new forces are at work. These forces are most pronounced and effective at the beginning of the new move - more power is needed to start a thing than to keep it going.

Some of my readers may think I am giving illustrations after these things happen on the tape, and that what a Tape Reader would have done at the time is problematical. I therefore wish to state that my tape illustrations are taken from the indications which actually showed themselves when they were freshly printed on the tape, at that time I did not know what was going to happen.

There are other ways in which a trader may employ himself during dull periods. One is to keep tab on the points of resistance in the leaders and play on them for fractional profits. This, we admit, is a rather precarious occupation, as the operating expenses constitute an extremely heavy percentage against the player, especially when the leading stocks only swing a point or so per day. But if one chooses to take these chances rather than be idle, the best way is to keep a chart on which should be recorded every fluctuation. This forms a picture of what is occurring and clearly defines the points of resistance, as well as the momentary trend.

In the following chart the stock opens at 181¼ and the first point of resistance is 181½. The first indication of a downward trend is shown in the dip to 181 1/8, and with these two straws showing the tendency, the Tape Reader goes short "at the market," getting, say, 181¼ (we'll give ourselves the worst of it). After making one more unsuccessful attempt to break through the resistance at 181½, the trend turns unmistakably downward, as shown by an almost and broken series of lower tops and bottoms.

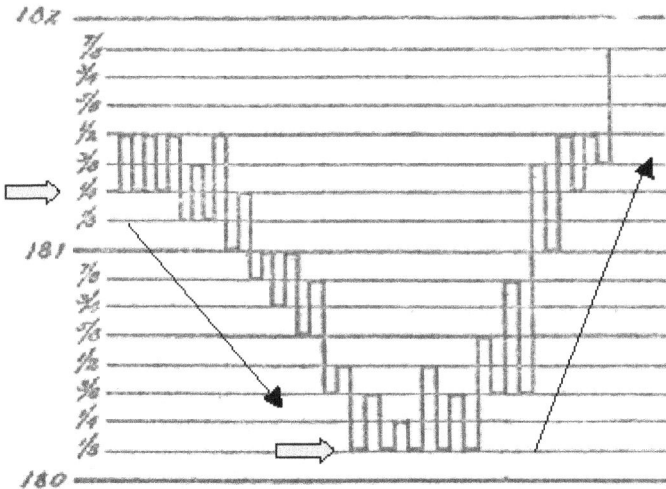

These indicate that the pressure is heavy enough to force the price to new low levels, and at the same time it is sufficient to prevent the rally going quite as high as on the previous bulge. At 180 1/8 a new point of resistance appears.

The decline is checked. The Tape Reader must cover and go long - the steps are now upward and as the price approaches the former point of resistance he watches it narrowly for his indication to close out.

This time, however, there is but slight opposition to the advance, and the price breaks through. He keeps his long stock. In making the initial trade he placed a "double" stop at 181 5/8 or 3/4, on the ground that if his stock overcame the resistance at 181 1/2 it would go higher and he would have to go with it. Being short 100 shares, his double stop order would read "Buy 200 at 181 5/8 stop". Of course the price might just catch his stop and go lower. These things will happen, and anyone who cannot face them without becoming perturbed had better learn self-control.

After going long around the low point, he should place another double stop at 180 or 179 7/8, for if the point of resistance is broken through after he has covered and gone long, he must switch his position in an instant. Not to do so would place him in the attitude of a guesser. If he is playing on this plan he must not dilute it with other ideas.

Remember this method is only applicable to a very dull market, and, as we have said, is precarious business. We cannot recommend it. It will not as a rule pay the Tape Reader to attempt scalping fractions out of the leaders in a dull market. Commissions, taxes and the invisible eighth, in addition to frequent losses, form too great a handicap. There must be wide swings if profits are to exceed losses. And the thing to do is wait for good opportunities. "The market is always with us" is an old and true saying. We are not compelled to trade and results do not depend on how often we trade, but on how much money we make.

There is another way of turning a dull market to good account, and that is by trading in the stocks which are temporarily active, owing to manipulative or other causes. The Tape Reader does not in the care a bit what sort of a label they put on the goods. Call a stock "Harlem Goats preferred" if you like, and make it active, preferably by means of manipulation, and the agile Tape Reader will trade in it with profit. It doesn't matters to him whether it's a railroad or a shooting gallery; whether it declares regular or "Irish" dividends; whether the abbreviation is X Y Z or Z Y X - so long as it furnishes indications and a broad liquid market on which to get in and out.

Take Beet Sugar on March 26, 1909, the day on which Union and Reading were so dull. It was easy to beat Beet Sugar. Even an embryo Tape Reader would have gone long at 30 or below, and as it never left him in doubt he could have dumped it at the top just before the close, or held it till the next day, when it touched 33½.

On March 5,1909, Kansas City Southern spent the morning drifting between 42 3/4 and 43 1/2. Shortly after the noon hour the stock burst into activity and large volume. Does any sane person suppose that a hundred or more people became convinced that Kansas City Southern was a purchase at that particular moment? What probably started the rise was the placing of manipulative orders, in which purchases predominated. Thus the sudden activity, the volume and the advancing tendency gave notice to the Tape Reader to "get aboard." The manipulator showed his hand and the "get aboard" Tape Reader had only to go long with the current.

The advance was not only sustained, but emphasized at certain points. Here the Tape Reader could have pyramided, using a stop close behind his average cost and raising it so as to conserve profits. If he bought his first lot at 44, his second at 45, and his third at 46, he could have thrown the whole at 46 5/8 and netted $406.50 for the day if he were trading in 100 share units, or $2,032.50 if trading in 50 share units.

CHAPTER EIGHT
The Use of Charts as Guides and Indicators

MANY interesting queries have been received regarding the use of charts. The following is a letter representative of most: "Referring to your figure chart explained in Volume 1 of the Magazine of Wall Street, I have found it a most valuable aid to detecting accumulation or distribution in market movements. I have been in Wall Street a number of years, and like many others have always shown a sceptical attitude toward charts and other mechanical methods of forecasting trends; but after a thorough trial of the chart on Union Pacific, I find that I could have made a very considerable sum if I had followed the indications shown. I note your suggestions to operators to study earnings, etc., and not to rely on charts, as they are very often likely to mislead. I regret that I cannot agree with you. You have often stated that the tape tells the story; since this is true, and a chart is but a copy of the tape, with indications of accumulation or distribution, as the case may be, why not follow the chart entirely, and eliminate all unnecessary time devoted to study of earnings, etc.?"

Let us consider those portions of the above which relate to Tape Reading, first clearly defining the difference between chart operations and tape reading. The genuine chart player usually operates in one stock at a time, using as a basis the past movements of that stock and following a more or less definite code of rules. He treats the market and his stock as a machine. He uses no judgment as to market conditions, and does not consider the movements of other stocks; but he exercises great discretion as to whether he shall "play" a chart signal or not. The Tape Reader operates on what the tape shows now. He is not wedded to any particular issue, and, if he chooses, can work without pencil, paper or memoranda of any sort. He also has his code of rules - less clearly defined than those of the chart player. So many different situations present themselves that his rules gradually become intuitive - a sort of second nature evolved by self-training and experience.

A friend to whom I have given some points in Tape Reading once asked if I had my rules all down so fine that I knew just which to use at certain moments. I answered him this way: "When you cross a street where the traffic is heavy, do you stop to consult a set of rules showing when to run ahead of a trolley car or when not to dodge a wagon? No. You take a look both ways and at the proper moment you walk across. Your mind may be on something else but your judgment tells you when to start and how fast to walk. That is the position of the trained Tape Reader". The difference between the Chart Player and the Tape Reader is therefore about as wide as between day and night.

But there are ways in which the Tape Reader may utilize charts as guides and indicators and for the purpose of reinforcing his memory. The Figure Chart is one of the best mechanical means of detecting accumulation and distribution. It is also valuable in showing the main points of resistance on the big swings. A figure chart cannot be made from the open, high, low and last prices, such as are printed in the average newspaper. We produced a Figure Chart of Amalgamated Copper showing movements during the 1903 panic and up to the following March (1904):

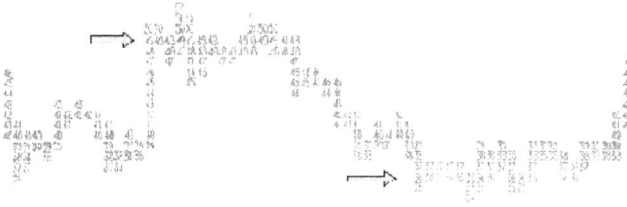

It makes an interesting study. The stock sold early in the year at 75 5/8 and the low point reached during the above period was 33 5/8. The movements prior to those recorded here show a series of downward steps, but when 36 is reached, the formation changes, and the supporting points are raised. A seven-point rally, a reaction to almost the low figure, and another sixteen-point rally follows. On this rally the lines 48-49 gradually form the axis and long rows of these figures seem to indicate that plenty of stock is for sale at this level. In case we are not sure as to whether this is further accumulation or distribution we wait until the price shows signs of breaking out of this narrow range. After the second run up to 51 the gradually lowering tops warn us that pressure is resumed. We therefore look for lower prices. The downward steps continue until 35 is touched, where a 36-7 line begins to form. There is a dip to 33 5/8, which gives us the full figure 34, after which the bottoms are higher and lines commence forming at 38-9. Here are all the earmarks of manipulative depression and accumulation - the stock is not allowed to rally over 39 until liquidation is complete. Then the gradually raised bottoms notify us in advance that the stock is about to push through to higher levels.

If the Figure Chart were an infallible guide no one would have to learn anything more than its correct interpretation in order to make big money. Our writer says, "after a thorough trial of the chart on U. P. I find that I could have made a very considerable sum if I had followed the indications shown". But he would not have followed the indications shown. He is fooling himself. It is easy to look over the chart afterwards and see where he could have made correct plays, but I venture to say he never tested the plan under proper conditions.

Let anyone, who thinks he can make money following a Figure Chart or any other kind of a chart have a friend prepare it, keeping secret the name of the stock and the period covered. Then put down on paper a positive set of rules which are to be strictly adhered to, so that there can be no guesswork. Each situation will then call for a certain play and no deviation is to be allowed. Cover up with a sheet of paper all but the beginning of the chart, gradually sliding the paper to the right as you progress. Record each order and execution just as if actually trading. Put my name down as covering the opposite side of every trade and when done send me a check for what you have lost. I have yet to meet the man who has made money trading on any kind of Chart over an extended period.

The Figure Chart can be used in other ways. Some people construct figure charts showing each fractional change

instead of full points. The idea may also be used in connection with the Dow Jones average prices. But for the practical
Tape Reader the full figure chart first described is about the
only one we can recommend. Its value to the Tape Reader
lies chiefly in its warnings of important moves thus putting
him on the watch for the moment when either process is
completed and the marking up or down begins. The chart
gives the direction of coming moves; the tape says "when."

The ordinary single line chart which is so widely used, is
valuable chiefly as a compact history of a stock's movements.
If the stock which is charted were the only one in the market,
its gyrations would be less erratic and its chart, therefore,
a more reliable indicator of its trend and destination. But
we must keep before us the incontrovertible fact that the
movements of every stock are to a greater or lesser extent
affected by those of every other stock. This in a large measure
accounts for the instability of stock movements as recorded
in single line charts. Then, too one stock may he the lever
with which the whole market is being held up, or the club
with which the general list is being pounded.

A chart of the pivotal stock might give a strong buying
indication, whereupon the blind chart devotee would go long
to his ultimate regret; for when the concealed distribution
was completed his stock would probably break quickly and
badly. This shows clearly the advantage of Tape Reading
over Charts. The Tape Reader sees everything that goes on;
chart player's vision is limited. Both aim to get in right and go
with the trend, but the eye that comprehends the market as
a whole is the one which can read this trend most accurately.

If one wishes a mechanical trend indicator as a supplement and a guide to his Tape Reading, he had best keep a chart composed of the average daily high and low of ten leading stocks in a group. First find the average high and average low for the day and make a chart showing which was touched first. This will be found a more reliable guide than the Dow Jones averages, which only consider the high, low and closing bid of each day, and which, as strongly illustrated in the May, 1901, panic, frequently do not fairly represent the day's actual fluctuations. Such a composite chart is of no value to the Tape Reader who scalps and closes out everything daily.

But it should benefit those who read the tape for the purpose of catching the important five or ten point moves. Such a trader will make no commitments not in accordance with the trend, as shown by this chart. His reason is that even a well planned bull campaign in a stock will not usually be pushed to completion in the face of a down trend in the general market. Therefore he waits until the trend conforms to his indication.

It seems hardly necessary to say that an up trend in any chart is indicated by consecutive higher tops and bottoms, like stairs going up, and the reverse by repeated steps toward a lower level. A series of tops or bottoms at the same level shows resistance. A protracted zigzag within a short radius accompanied by very small volume means lifelessness, but with normal or abnormally large volume, accumulation or distribution is more or less evidenced. Here is a style of hand chart especially adapted to the study of volumes:

51
7/8
3/4
5/8
1/2
3/8
1/4
1/8
50

(6) (9)
(11) (5) (3) (8)
(4) (2)   (4)
(2)   (10)
(5)   (8)
(7) (7) (7)
(3) (16)
(1)
(10)

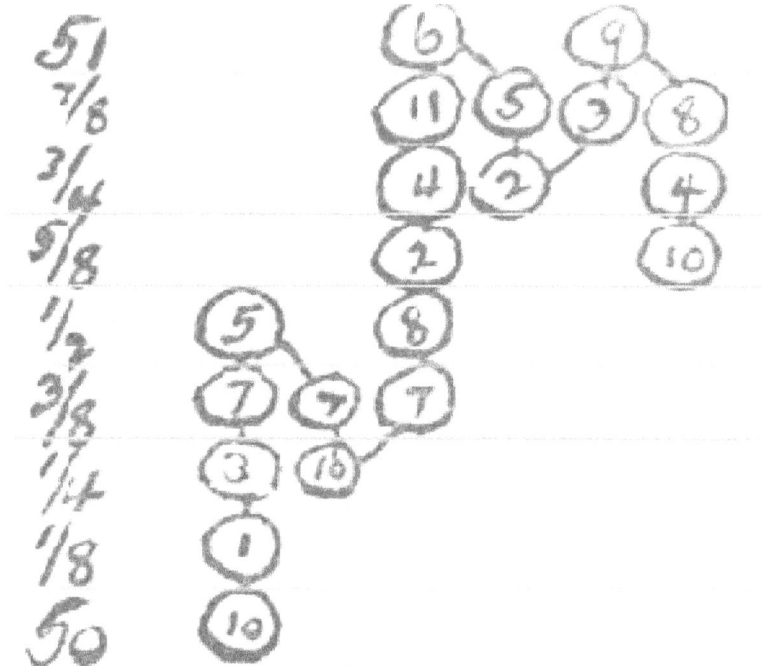

When made to cover a day's movements in a stock, this chart is particularly valuable in showing the quantity of stock at various levels. Figures represent the total 100 share lots at the respective fractions. Comparisons are ready made by adding the quantities horizontally. Many other suggestions may be derived from the study of this chart. The proficient Tape Reader will doubtless prefer to discard all mechanical helps, because they interfere with his sensing the trend. Besides, if he keeps the charts himself the very act of running them distracts his attention from the tape on which his eye should be constantly riveted.

This can of course be overcome by employing an assistant; but taking everything into consideration - the division of attention, the contradictions and the confusing situations which will frequently result - we advise students to stand free of mechanical helps so far as it is possible. Our correspondent in saying "a chart is but a copy of the tape" doubtless refers to the chart of one stock. The full tape cannot possibly be charted. The tape does tell the story, but charting one or two stocks is like recording the actions of one individual as exemplifying the actions of a very large family.

CHAPTER NINE

Daily Trading Versus Longer Term Trading

JUST now I took a small triangular piece of blotting paper three-eighths of an inch at its widest, and stuck it on the end of a pin. I then threw a blot of ink on a paper and put the blotter into contact. The ink fairly jumped up into the blotter, leaving the paper comparatively dry.

This is exactly how the market acts on the tape when its absorptive powers are greater than the supply - large quantities are taken at the offered prices and at the higher levels. Prices leap forward. The demand seems insatiable. After two or three blots had thus been absorbed, the blotter would take no more. It was thoroughly saturated. Its demands were satisfied. Just in this way the market comes to a standstill at the top of a rise and hangs there. Supply and demand are equalized at the new price level.

Then I filled my pen with ink, and let the fluid run off the point and onto the blotter. (This illustrated the distribution of stocks in the market). Beyond a certain point the blotter would take no more. A drop formed and fell to the paper. (Supply exceeded demand). The more I put on the blotter the faster fell the drops. (Liquidation - market seeking a lower level). This is a simple way of fixing in our minds the principal opposing forces that are constantly operating in the market-absorption and distribution, demand and supply, support and pressure. The more adept a Tape Reader becomes in weighing and measuring these elements, the more successful he will be. But he must remember that even his most accurate readings will often be nullified by events that are transpiring every moment of the day. His stock may start upward with a rush-apparently with power enough to carry it several points; but after advancing a couple of points it may run up against a larger quantity of stock than can be absorbed or some unforeseen incident may change the whole complexion of the market.

To show how an operator may be caught twice on the wrong side in one day and still come out ahead, let us look at the tape of December 21, 1908. Union Pacific opened below the previous night's close: 500 @ 179 6000 @ 178 3/4 ...and for the first few moments looked as though there was some inside support. Supposing the Tape Reader had bought 100 Union Pacific at 178 7/8, he would have soon noticed fresh selling orders in sufficient volume to produce weakness. Upon this he would have immediately sold 200 Union Pacific at 178¼, putting him short one hundred at the latter price. The weakness increased and after a drive to 176 1/2, two or three warnings were given that the pressure was temporarily off. A comparatively strong undertone developed in Southern Pacific as well as other stocks and short covering began in Union Pacific, which came 600 @ 176 5/8 1000 @ 176 ¾ ... then 177¼. Assuming that the operator considered this the turn, he would have, bought 200 Union Pacific at 176 7/8, which was the next quotation. This would have put him long.

Thereafter the market showed more resiliency, but only small lots appeared on the tape.

A little later the market quiets down. The rally does not hold well. He expects the stock to react again to the low point. This it does, but it fails to halt there; it goes driving through to 176, accompanied by considerable weakness in the other active stocks. This is his indication that fresh liquidation has started. So he, sells 200 Union Pacific at 176 That is, he dumps over his long stock and goes short at 176. The weakness continues and there is no sign of a rally until after the stock his struck 174 1/2. This being a break of 6¼ points since yesterday, the Tape Reader is now wide awake for signs of a turn, realizing that every additional fraction brings him nearer to that point, wherever it may be. After touching 174 1/2 the trend of the market changes completely. Larger lots are in demand at the offered prices. There is a final drive but very little stock comes out on it. During this drive he, buys 100 Union Pacific at 175 7/8, and as signs of a rally multiply he buys 100 at 175 1/4 From that moment it is easy sailing. There is ample opportunity for him to unload his last purchase just before the close when he sells 100 at 176 5/8.

Bought	Sold	Loss	Profit
178 7/8	178 1/4	62.50	-
176 7/8	178 1/4	-	137.50
176 7/8	176	87.50	-
174 7/6	176	-	112.50
175 1/4	176 5/8	-	137.50
	Commissions & Taxes	135.00	-
	Totals	285.00	387.50
	Less Loss	-285.00	
	Net Profit For Day		$102.50

This is doing very well considering he was caught twice on the wrong side and in his anxious trading paid $135.00 in commissions and taxes. Success in trading comes down to a question of reducing and eliminating losses, commissions, interest and taxes.

Let us see whether he might have used better judgment. His first trade seems to have been made on what appeared to be inside buying. No trend had developed. He saw round lots being taken at 178 3/4 and over and reasoned that a rally should naturally follow pronounced support. His mistake was in not waiting for a clearly defined trend. If waiting for the buying was strong enough to absorb all offerings and turn the market, he would have done better to have waited until this was certain. When a stock holds steady within a half point radius it does not signify a reversal of trend, but rather a halting place from which a new move in either direction may begin. Had he followed the first sharp move, his original trade would have been on the short not the long side. This would have saved him his first loss with its attendant expenses, aggregating $89.50, and would have nearly doubled the day's profits.

His second loss was made on a trade which involved one of the finest points in the art of Tape Reading - that of distinguishing a rally from a change in trend. A good way to do this successfully is to figure where a stock is due to come after it makes an upturn, allowing that a normal rally is from one-half to two-thirds of the decline. That is, when a stock declines two and a half points we can look for at least a point and a quarter rally unless the pressure is still on. In case the decline is not over, the rally will fall short. What did Union do after it touched 176½? It sold at 176 5/8 – 177 ¾ - 177 ¼ . Having declined from 179 1/8 to 176 ½, 2 5/8 points, it was due to rally at least 1¼ points, or to 177 ¾ . Its failing to make this figure indicated that the decline was not over and that his short position should be maintained. Also, that last jump of half a point between sales showed an unhealthy condition of the market. For a few moments there was evidently a cessation of selling, then somebody reached for a hundred shares offered at 177¼. As the next sale was 176 7/8 the hollowness of the rise became apparent. While this rally lasted, the lots were small. This of itself was reason for not covering. Had a genuine demand sprung from either longs or shorts a steady rise, on increasing volumes, would have taken place. The absence of such indications seems to us now a reason for not covering and going long at 176 7/8.

It is very difficult for anyone to say what he would actually have done under the circumstances, but had both these trades been avoided for the reasons mentioned, the profit for the day would have been $421, as the 100 sold at 178 1/4 would have been covered at 174 7/8, and the long at 175 1/4 sold out at 176 5/8. So we can see the advantage of studying our losses and mistakes, with a view to benefiting in future transactions.

As previously explained, the number of dollars profit is subordinate to whether the trader can make profits at all and whether the points made exceed the points lost. With success from this standpoint it is only a question of increased capital enabling one to enlarge his trading unit. A good way to watch the progress of an account is to keep a book showing dates, quantities, prices, profits and losses, also commission, tax and interest charges. Beside each trade should be entered the number of points net profit or loss, together with a running total showing just how many points the account is ahead or behind. A chart of these latter figures will prevent anyone fooling himself as to his progress. People are too apt to remember their profits and forget their losses. The losses taken by an expert Tape Reader are so small that he can trade in much larger units than one who is away from the tape or who is trading with an arbitrary stop. The Tape Reader will seldom take over half a point to a point loss for the reason that he will generally buy or sell at, or close to, the pivotal point or the line of resistance. Therefore, should the trend of his stock suddenly reverse, he is with it in a moment.

The losses in the above mentioned Union Pacific transactions (5/8 and 7/8 respectively) are perhaps a fair average, but frequently he will be able to trade with a risk of only ¼, 3/8, or ½ point. The fact that this possible loss is confined to a fraction should not lead him to trade too frequently. It is better to look on part of the time; to rest the mind and allow the judgment to clarify. Dull days will often constrain one for a time and are therefore beneficial. The big money in Tape Reading is made during very active markets. Big swings and large volumes produce unmistakable indications and a harvest for the experienced operator.

He welcomes twenty, thirty and fifty-point moves in stocks like Reading, Union or Consolidated Gas-powerful plays by financial giants. And this fact reminds us: Is it better to close trades each day, or hold through reactions, and if necessary, for several days or weeks in order to secure a large profit? The answer to this question depends somewhat upon the temperament of the Tape Reader. If his make-up be such that he can closely follow the small swings with profit, gradually becoming more expert and steadily increasing his commitments, he will shortly "arrive" by that route.

If his nerves are such that he cannot trade in and out actively, but is content to wait for big opportunities and patient enough to hold on for large profits, he will also "get there." It is impossible to say which style of trading would produce the best average results, because it depends alto-gether upon individual qualifications, attitudes and tolerance of risk. Looking at the question broadly, we should say that the Tape Reader who understood the lines thus far suggested in this series, might find it both difficult and less profitable to operate solely for the long swings. In the first place, he would be obliged to let twenty or thirty opportunities pass by to every one that he would accept. The small swings of one to three points greatly outnumber the five and ten-point movements, and there would be a considerable percentage of losing trades no matter how he operated.

Many of the indications, such as the extent of reactions, lines of resistance, etc., will be found equally operative in the broader swings, just as an enlargement of a photograph retains the lines of its original. Tape Reading seems essentially a profession for the person who is mentally active and flexible, capable of making quick and accurate decisions and keenly sensitive to the smallest and almost imperceptible signals and indications.

On the other hand, trading for the larger swings requires one to ignore the minor indications and to put some stress upon the influential news of the day, and its effect upon sentiment; he must stand ready to take larger losses and in many ways handle himself in a manner altogether different from that of the day trader. The more closely we look at the differences between the longer-term trader/investor and the day trader, the more the two methods of operating seem to disunite, the long-term investing player appearing best adapted to those who are not in continuous touch with the market and who therefore have the advantage of distance and perspective.

There is no reason why the Tape Reader should not make long-term trading an auxiliary profit producer if he can keep such trades from influencing his daily operations. For example, in the previously mentioned shake-down in

Reading from 144 3/8 to 118, on his first buying indication he could have taken on an extra lot for the long swing, knowing that if the turn had really been made, a rally to over 130 was due. A stop order would have limited his risk and conserved his profits as they rolled up and there is no telling how much of the subsequent forty point rise he might been able to ride.

Another case was when Steel broke from 58 3/4 (November, 1908) to 41¼ in February. The market at the time was hinging on Steel and it was likely that the Tape Reader would be operating in it. His first long trade under this plan would be for at least a hundred shares more than his usual amount, with a stop on the long pull lot at say 40 3/4. He would naturally expect a rally of at least 8 3/4 points (to 50), but would, in a sense, forget this hundred shares, so long as the market showed no signs of another important decline. When it reached 60 he might still be holding it.

The above are merely a couple of opportunities. Dozens of such show themselves every year and should form no small part of the Tape Reader's income. But he must separate such trades from his regular daily trading; to allow them to conflict with each other would destroy the effectiveness of both. If he finds the long pull trade interfering with the accuracy of his judgment, he should close it out at once. He must play on one side of the fence if he cannot operate on both. You can readily foresee how a trader with one hundred shares of Steel at 43 for the long-term, and two hundred for the day, would be tempted to close out all three hundred on indications of a decline. This is where he can test his ability to act in a dual capacity. He must ask himself: Have I good reason for thinking Steel will sell down five points before up five? Is this a small reaction or a big shake-down? Are we still in a bull swing? Has the stock had its normal rally from the last decline? These and many other questions will enable him to decide whether he should hold this hundred shares or "clean house."

It takes an exceptionally strong will and clear head to act in this way without interfering with your regular trading. Anyone can sell two hundred and hold one hundred; but will his judgment be biased because he is simultaneously long and short–bullish and bearish? There's the problem! The real Day Trader is more likely to prefer a clean slate at market closing every day, so that he can sit down to his ticker at the next morning's opening and say, "I have no commitments and no opinion. I will follow the first strong indication." He would rather average $100 a day for ten days than make $1,000 on one trade in the same length of time.

The risk is generally limited to a fraction and having arrived at a point where he is showing even small average daily profits, his required capital per 100 shares need not be over $1,500 to $2,000. Suppose for sixty days on 100 share a day trading his average profits over losses were only a quarter of a point – or $25 a day. At the end of that time his capital would have been increased by $1,500, enabling him to trade in 200 share lots. Another thirty days with similar results and he could trade in 300 share lots, and so on. I don't mention these figures for any other purpose than to again emphasize that the objective point in Tape Reading is not large individual profits, but a continuous chipping in of small average net profits per day.

Some time ago, I am told, a man from the West Coast came into my office and said that he had been impressed by this series on Tape Reading, and had come to New York for the sole purpose of trying his hand at it. He had $1,000 which he was willing to lose in demonstrating whether he was fitted for the work. I was later informed that he called again and related some of his experiences. It seems that he could not abstain from trading, but started within two or three days after he decided on a brokerage house. He stated that during the two months he had made forty-two trades of ten shares each and had never had on hand over twenty full shares at any one time. He admitted that he had frequently mixed guesswork and tips with his Tape Reading but as a rule he had followed the tape.

His losses were seldom over a point and his greatest loss was one and a half points. His maximum profit was three points. He had at times traded in other stocks beside the leaders. In spite of his inexperience, and his attempt to mix tips and guess with shrewd judgment, he was ahead of the game, after paying commissions, taxes, etc. This was especially surprising in view of the trader's market through which be had passed. While the amount of his net profit was small, the fact that he had shown any profit during this study period was reason enough for congratulations.

Another handicap which he did not perhaps realize was his environment. He had been trading in an office where he could hear and see what everyone else was doing, and where news, gossip and opinions were freely and openly expressed by many people. All these things tended to influence him, and to switch him from his foundation in Tape Reading fundamentals to other methods but he is persisting and shows some signs of discipline. I have no doubt that having mastered the art of cutting losses and keeping commitments down and returning to Tape Reading fundamentals, he will soon overcome his other deficiencies and begin showing remarkable progress. Given a broad, active market, he should show increasing average daily profits. Speculation is a business. It must he learned.

CHAPTER TEN

Various Examples and Suggestions

RECENT trading observations and experiments have convinced me that it is impracticable and almost impossible to gauge the extent of a move by its initial fluctuations. Many important swings begin in the most modest way. The top of an important decline may present nothing more than a light volume and a drifting tendency toward lower prices, subsequently developing into a heavy, slumpy market, and ending in a violent downward plunge. If it has been moving within a three-point radius and suddenly takes on new life and activity, bursting through its former bounds, he must go with it. I do not mean that he should try to catch every wiggle. If the stock rises three points and then reverses one or one and a half points on light volume, he must look upon it as a perfectly natural reaction and not a change of trend. The expert operator will not ordinarily let all of three points get away from him. He will keep pushing his stop up behind until the first good reaction puts him out at close to the high figure. Having purchased at such a time, he will sell out again as the price once more approaches the high figure, unless indications point to its forging through to a new high level.

The more we study volumes, the better we appreciate their value in Tape Reading. It frequently occurs that a stock will work within a three-point range for days at a time without giving one a chance for a respectable-sized 'scalp'. Without going out of these boundaries, it suddenly begins coming out on the tape in thousands instead of hundreds. This is evidence that a new movement has started, but not necessarily in the direction first indicated. The Tape Reader must immediately go with the trend, but until it is clearly defined and the stock breaks its former limits with large and increasing volumes, he must use caution. The reason is this: If the stock has been suddenly advanced, it may be for the purpose of facilitating sales by a large operator.

The best way to distinguish the genuine from the fictitious move is to watch out for abnormally large volumes within a small radius. This is usually evidence of manipulation. The large volume is simply a means of attracting buyers and disguising the hand of the operator. A play of this kind took place when Reading struck 159 3/4 in June1909. I counted some 80,000 shares within about half a point of 159 - unmistakable notice of a coming decline. This was a case where the stock was put up before being put down, and the Tape Reader who interpreted the move correctly and played for a good down swing would have made considerable money.

We frequently hear people complaining that "the public is not in this market," as though that were a reason why stocks should not go up or the market should be avoided. The speaker is usually one of those who constitute "the public," but he regards the expression as signifying "every outsider except myself." In the judgment of many the market is better off without the public. To be sure, brokers do not enjoy so large a business, the fluctuations are not so riotous, but the market moves in an orderly way and responds more accurately to prevailing conditions. A market in which the general pubic predominates the purchase of individual stocks represents a sort of speculative "jag" indulged in by those whose stock market knowledge should be rated at 1/8's.

Everyone recognizes the fact that when the smoke clears away, the Street is full of victims who didn't know how and couldn't wait to learn. Their buying and selling produce violent fluctuations, however, and in this respect are of advantage to the Tape Reader who would much rather see ten-point than three-point swings. To offset this, there are some disadvantages. First, in a market where there is "rioting of accumulated margins," the tape is so far behind that it is seldom one can secure an execution at anywhere near his price. This is especially true when activity breaks out in a stock which has been comparatively dull. So many people with money, watching the tape, are attracted by these apparent opportunities, that the scramble to get in results in every one paying more than he figured; thus the Tape Reader finds it impossible to know where he is at until he gets his report. His tape prices are five minutes behind and his broker is so busy it takes four or five minutes for an execution instead of seconds. In the next place, stop orders are often filled at from small fractions to points away from his stop price-there is no telling what figure he will get, while in ordinary markets he can place his stops within ¼ of a resistance point and frequently have the price come within 1/8 of his stop without catching it.

Speaking of stop orders, the ways in which one may

manipulate his stops for protection and advantage, become more numerous as experience is acquired. If the Tape Reader is operating for a fractional average profit per trade, or per day, he cannot afford to let a point profit run into a loss, or fail to "plug" a larger profit at a point where at least a portion of it will be preserved.

One of my recent day's trading will illustrate this idea. I had just closed out a couple of trades, in which there had been losses totalling slightly over a point. Both were on the long side. The market began to show signs of a break, and singling out Reading as the most vulnerable, I got short at 150 3/4. In a few moments it sold below 150. My stop was moved down so there couldn't be a loss, and soon a slight rally and another break gave me a new stop that insured a profit. A third drive started, and I pushed the stop down to within 1/4 of the tape price at the time, as it was late in the day and I considered this the final plunge. By the time my order reached the floor the price was well away from this latest stop and when the selling became most violent I told my broker to cover "at the market." The price paid was within 1/4 of the bottom for the day, and netted 2 5/8 after commissions were paid.

I strongly advocate this method of profit insuring. It is also a question whether, in such a case, the trade had better not be stopped out than closed out. When you push a stop close behind a rise or a decline, you leave the way open for a further profit; but when you close the trade of your own volition, you shut off all such chances. If it is your habit to close out everything before market close daily, the stop may be placed closer than ordinarily during the last fifteen minutes of the session, and when a sharp move in the desired direction occurs the closing out may be done by a stop only a fraction away from the extreme price.

This plan of using stops is a sort of squeezing out the last drop of profit from each trade and never losing any part that can possibly be retained. Suppose the operator sells a stock short at 53 and it breaks to 51. He is foolish not to bring his stop down to 51¼ unless the market is ripe for a heavy decline. With his stop at this point he has two chances out of three that the result will be satisfactory: 1) The price may go lower and yield a further profit; 2) The normal rally to 52 will catch his stop and enable him to put the stock out again at that price; 3) The stock will rally to about 51 ¼, catch his stop and then go lower. But he can scarcely mourn over the loss of a further profit. If the stock refuses to rally the full point to which it is entitled, that is, if it comes up to 51½ or 5/8 and still acts heavy, it may be expected to break lower, and there usually is ample time to get short again at a price that will at least cover commissions.

There is nothing more confusing than to attempt scalping on both sides of the market at once. You might go long of a stock which is being put up or is going up for some special reason, and short of another stock which is persistently weak. Both trades may pan out successfully, but in the meantime your judgment will be interfered with and some foolish mistakes will be made in four cases out of five. As Dickson G. Watts said, "Act so as to keep the mind clear, the judgment trustworthy." The mind is not clear when the trader is working actively on two opposing sides of the market. A bearish indication is favourable to one trade, and unfavourable to the other. He finds himself interpreting every development as being to his advantage and forgetting the important fact that he is also on the opposite side. If you are short of one stock and see another that looks like a purchase, it is much better to wait until you have covered your short trade (on a dip if possible), and then take the long side of the other issue.

The best time for both covering and going long is on a recession that in such a case serves a double purpose. The mind should he made up in advance as to which deal offers the best chance for profit, so that when the moment for action arrives there will he nothing to do but act. This is one great advantage the Tape Reader has over other operators who do not employ market science. By a process of elimination he decides which side of the market and which stock affords the best opportunity. He either gets in at the inception of a movement or waits for the first reaction after the move has started. He knows just about where his stock should come on the reaction and judges by the way it then acts whether his first impression is confirmed or contradicted. After he gets in it must act up to expectations or he should abandon the trade and get out of it immediately. If it is a bull move, the volume must increase and the rest of the market offer some support or at least not oppose it. The reactions must show a smaller volume than the advances, indicating light pressure, and each upward swing must be of longer duration and reach a new high level, or it will mean that the rise has spent its force either temporarily or finally.

Tape Reading is the only known method of trading which

gets you in at the beginning, keeps you posted throughout the move, and gets you out when it has culminated. Has anyone ever heard of a man, method, system, or anything else that will do this for you in Wall Street? It has made fortunes for the comparatively few who have followed it. It is an art in which one can become highly expert and more and more successful as experience sharpens his instincts and judgment and shows him what to avoid.

CHAPTER ELEVEN

Obstacles To Be Overcome - Potential Profits

MENTAL poise is an indispensable factor in Tape Reading. The mind should be absolutely free to concentrate upon the work; there should be no feeling that certain things are to be accomplished within a given time; no fear, anxiety, or greed.

When a Tape Reader has his emotions well in hand, he will play as though the game were dominoes.

When anything interferes with this attitude it should be eliminated. If, for example, there be an unusual series of losses, the trader had better suspend operations until he discovers the cause.

The following are the Tape Readers 7 Commandments:

1. Do not overtrade ! One may be trading too often. Many opportunities for profit develop from each day's movements; only the very choicest should he acted upon. There should be no haste. The market will be there to-morrow in case to-day's opportunities do not meet requirements.

2. Eliminate anxiety! Anxiety to make a record, to avoid losses, to secure a certain profit for the day or period will

greatly warp the judgment, and lead to a low percentage of profits. Tape Reading is a good deal like laying eggs. If the hen is not left to pick up the necessary food and retire in peace to her nest, she will not produce properly. If she is worried by dogs and small boys, or tries to lay seven eggs out of material for six, the net proceeds may be an omelette. The Tape Reader's profits should develop naturally. He should buy or sell because it is the thing to do - not because he wants to make a profit or fears to make a loss.

3. Don't trade when the market isn't acting right! The market may be unsuited to Tape Reading operations. When prices drift up and down without trend, like a ship without a rudder, and few positive indications develop, the percentage of losing trades is apt to be high. When this condition continues it is well to hold off until the character of the market changes.

4. Get a broker you can trust! One's broker may be giving poor service. In a game as fine as this, every fraction – every second counts. Executions of market orders should average not over one minute. Stop orders should be reported in less time as such orders are on the floor and at the proper post when they become operative. By close attention to details in the handling of my orders, I have been able to reduce the average time of my executions to less than one minute. The quickest report obtained thus far required but 25 seconds. A considerable portion of my orders are executed in from thirty to forty seconds, varying according to whether my broker is near the phone or in a distant crowd when the orders reach

the floor and how far the identical "crowd" is from his 'phone.

5. Do not leave orders to the discretion of the broker! Make your orders clear and firm. Do not say, "Try to sell better than the bid and let me know what happened" – say, "Sell at the bid price and report instantly!" He cannot "do better" than the momentary bid or offered price. Ordinarily it is expected and is really an advantage to the general run of speculators to have the broker use some discretion; that is, try to do better, providing there is no chance of losing his market. But I do not wish my broker to act like that for me. My indications usually show me the exact moment when a stock should be bought or sold under this method, and a few moments' delay often means a good many dollars lost. With the execution of orders reduced to a matter of seconds, I can also hold stop orders in my own hands and when the stop price is reached, phone the order to buy or sell at the market. Results are very satisfactory as my own broker handles the orders and not the specialist or some other floor broker.

6. Keep alert, calm after losses! The Tape Reader should be careful to trade only in such amounts as will not interfere with his judgment. If he finds that a series of losses upsets him it is an easy matter to reduce the number of shares to one-half or one-quarter of the regular amount, or even to ten shares, so that the dollars involved are no longer a factor. This gives him a chance for a little self-examination.

7. Stay physically and mentally fit! If a person is in poor

physical condition or his mental alertness below par for any reason, he may be unable to stand the excitement attending the work. Dissipation, for example, may render one unfit to carry all the quotations in his head, or to plan and execute his moves quickly and accurately. When anything of this kind occurs which prevents the free play of all the faculties it is best to bring the day's work to a close.

Some of my readers may think it futile to aim for a fractional average profit per trade when there are many full points per day to be made by holding on through days and weeks and getting full benefit of the big moves. Admitting that it is possible to make many more points at times, there is a risk of losses corresponding to the profits and the question is not how much we can make, but how much we can make net. Tape Reading reduces profit- making to a manufacturing basis. To show how the nimble eighths pile up when their cumulative power is fully employed, I have prepared a table representing the results of 250 trading days, starting with a capital of $1,000. It is assumed that the Tape Reader has reached that stage of expertness where he can average one trade a day and a profit of $12.50 per trade, and that as fast as $1,000 is accumulated he adds 100 shares to his trading unit.

These results depend solely upon the Tape Reader's ability to make more than he loses per day. There is no limit to the number of shares he can trade in, provided he has the margin. If he is at all proficient his margin will not be depleted more than a few points before he makes up his losses and more. He is not pyramiding in the ordinary sense of the word; he is simply doing an increasing volume of shares as his capital expands. All progressive business men increase commitments as fast as warranted by their capital and opportunities. What a profit 1/8 of point per day would amount to in 250 days if profits were used as additional margin:

100 Shares at $12.50 Per Day = $1,000.00 in 80 days

200 Shares $25 $1,000.00 in 40 days (Etc)

300 Shares $37.50 $1,012.50 27

400 Shares $50.00 $1,000.00 20

500 Shares $62.50 $1,000.00 16

600 Shares $75.00 $1,050.00 14

700 Shares $87.50 $1,050.00 12

800 Shares $100.00 $1,000.00 10

900 Shares $112.50 $1,012.50 9

1000 Shares $125.00 $1000.00 8

1100 Shares $137.50 $962.50 7

1200 Shares $150.00 $1050.00 7

GROSS $12,137.50 in 250 Days

Less Tax & Commissions -$1,942.00

Net Profit $10,195.50

Assuming that there are about three hundred Stock Exchange sessions in the year, the two hundred and fifty days figured represent five-sixths of a year, or ten months. From that time on, having struck his gait, the Tape Reader can, without increasing his unit to over 1200 shares, make $900 a week or $46,800 a year.

One trader who for years has been trying to scalp the market and who could never quite secure a profit, reports that his first attempts at applying these rules resulted in a loss of about $20 per trade. This he gradually reduced to $12, then to $8, finally succeeding in throwing the balance over to the credit side and is now able to make a daily profit of from $12 to $30 per 100 shares. That's only an example of small traders. A medium size traders goal should be to make $150 to $350 per 1000 shares. This is doing very well indeed. I have no doubt that profits will continue to increase as experience increases.

Some people seem to hold the opinion that as the profits desired are only 1/8 average per trade one should limit himself in taking profits. Perhaps I have not made myself clear. I buy and sell when I get my indications. In going into a trade

I do not know whether it will show a profit or a loss, or how much. I try to trade at a point where I can secure protection with a stop from ¼ to ½ point away, so that my risk is limited to this fraction plus commission and tax. If the trade goes in my favour I push the stop up as soon as possible, to a point where there can be no loss. I do not let profits run blindly but only so long as there appears no indication on which to close. No matter where my stop order stands, I am always on the watch for danger signals. Sometimes I get them away in advance of the time a trade should be closed; in other instances my "get out" will flash onto the tape as suddenly and as clearly defined as a streak of lightning against a black sky. When the tape says "get out" I never stop to calculate how much profit or loss I have or whether I am ahead or behind on the day.

I strive for an increasing average profit but I do not keep my eye so much on the fraction or points made or lost, so much as on myself and keeping alert. I endeavour to perfect myself in resolute calmness and precision, quickness of thought, accuracy of judgment, promptness in planning and executing my trades, foresight, intuition, courage and initiative. Masterful control of myself in these respects will produce a winning average - it is merely a question of practice.

To show how accurately the method works out in practice, I will describe one recent day's trading in which there were three transactions, involving six orders (three buying and three selling). The market didn't go one-eighth against me in five orders out of the six. In the sixth, the stock went 5/8 above the selling price at which my order was given.

Here are the details: I had no open trades at the market's open bell. Kansas City Southern, which had been intensely dull, came on the tape 2600 at 46 3/4. I gave a buying order and before it could reach the "post" the Tape said 46 7/8 and 47. The stock rose steadily and after selling at 48 5/8 and coming back to 48 1/2 I gave the selling order. It did not touch 48 5/8 again.

The next trade was in Reading. I saw that it was being held in check in spite of its great strength. The stock had opened at 158. After a certain bulge I saw the reaction coming. When it arrived, and the stock was selling at 157 1/2, I gave the buying order, and got mine at 157 5/8. It immediately rose to 158 3/4. I noted selling indications and gave the order while the stock was at that price on the tape. It did not react sufficiently to warrant my picking it up again and later went to 159 3/8, which was 5/8 above my selling indication.

Southern Pacific suddenly loomed up as a winner and I bought it at 135. It promptly went to 135 1/2. The rest of the market began to look temporarily over-bulled, so I gave my order to sell when the stock was 135 1/2, which proved to be the highest for the day, making the fifth time out of six orders when my stock moved almost instantly in my favour.

This illustration is given as an example of the high per-centage of accuracy possible under this method of trading. I do not pretend to be able to accomplish these results except occasionally, but I am constantly striving to do so in a large percentage of my trades. If one makes 2 3/8 points one day and loses 2 points in the next two days, he is 3/8 ahead for the three days, or an average of 1/8 per day. He may have losing and winning streaks, get discouraged and lose his nerve at times, but if he is made of the right stuff he will in time overcome all obstacles and land at the desired goal.

CHAPTER TWELVE
Closing The Trade

THE student of Tape Reading, especially he who puts his knowledge into actual practice, is constantly evolving new ideas and making discoveries which modify his former methods. From each new elevation he enjoys a broader view; what were obstacles disappear; his problems gradually simplify.

We have previously defined Tape Reading as the art of determining the immediate trend of prices. If one can do this successfully in the majority of his trades, his profits should roll up. But recognizing the trend and getting in at the right moment is only one-half of the business. Knowing when to close a trade is just as important if not the most important part of a complete transaction. At a certain point in my trading, I became aware that a large percentage of my losing trades resulted from failure to close at the culmination of what I have termed the immediate trend.

An example will make this clear: New York Central was on a certain day the strongest stock in a bull market that showed a tendency to react. The pressure was on Reading and Steel. My indications were all bullish, so I couldn't consistently sell either of the latter short. I was looking for an opportunity to buy. The market began to slide off, Reading and Steel being the principal clubs with which the pounding was done. I watched them closely and the moment I saw that the selling of these two stocks had ceased, gave my order to buy New York Central, getting it at 137 1/4. It never touched there again, and in ten minutes was 139 bid for 5,000 shares. Here I should have sold, as my buying indication was for that particular advance. Especially should I have sold when I saw the rise culminate in a spectacular bid which looked like bait for outside buyers. Of course the stock might have gone higher The main trend for the day was upward. But for the time being 139 was the high point. I knew the stock was due to react from this figure, and it did, but at the bottom of the normal reaction selling broke out in fresh quarters and the whole market came down heavily. The result was that my profit was only a fraction of what it ought to have been. This is the way the trade might have been made: I should have sold when 139 was noisily bid, and when the reaction had run its course, picked it up again, provided indications were still bullish. If they were not I would have been in the position of looking to get short instead of waiting for a chance to get out of my long.

Having reserved in the early part of this book the right to revise my views, I will here record the claim that the best results in active Tape Reading lie in recognizing the moves as they occur, getting in when they start and out when they culminate. This will in most cases cause failure to get all of the moves in the one most active stock for the day, but should result in many small profits, and I believe the final results will exceed those realized by sitting through reactions with any one stock. There is a very wide difference in mental thought processes between the man who feels compelled to get out of something and one who has money to invest and is looking for a chance to make a fresh trade.

The start and finish of a small move is best illustrated by a triangle - the narrow end representing the beginning, and the wide end the termination of the move.

The width in an upward move would appear like this:

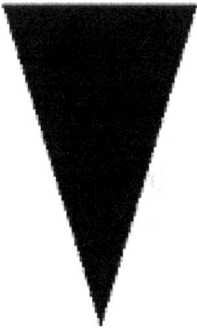

and a downward move like this:

These figures denote the widening character of a move as it progresses and are intended to show how volume, activity and number of transactions expand until, at the end, comparatively active conditions prevail. The principle works the same in the larger market moves; witness the spectacular rise in Union Pacific within a few sessions marking the end of the August1 1909, boom.

After closing out a trade the tape will tell on the following reaction whether you are justified in taking the same stock on again or whether some other issue will pay better. Frequently a stock will be seen preparing for a move two or three swings ahead of the one in which it becomes the leader. This is a fine point, but with study and practice the most complicated indications clarify.

And now a word about you – you who are endeavouring to turn day trading to practical account. The results which are attainable depend solely upon the YOU. Each must work out his own method of trading, based on suggestions derived from these suggestions or from other sources.

It will doubtless be found that what is one man's meat is another's poison, and that no amount of "book learning" will be of any use if the student does not put his knowledge to an actual test in the market. It is surprising how any familiarity with subjects relative to the stock market, but seemingly having no bearing upon Tape Reading, will lead to opportunities or aid in making deductions. And so when asked what books will best for supplementing these suggestions, I should say: Read everything you can get hold of. If you find but a single idea in a publication it is well worth the time and money spent in procuring and studying it.

Wall Street is crowded with men who are there in the hope of making money, but who cannot be persuaded to look at the proposition from a practical business standpoint. Least of all will they study it, for this means long hours of hard work, and Mr. Speculator is laziness personified. Frequently I have met those who pin their faith to some one point, such as the volumes up or down, and call it Tape Reading. Others, unconsciously trading on mechanical indications such as charts, pretend to be reading the market. Then there is a class of people who read the tape with their tongues, calling off each transaction, a certain accent on the higher or lower quotations indicating whether they are bullish or bearish.

These and others in their class are merely operating on the superficial. If they would spend the same five or six hours a day (which they now practically waste) in close study of the business of speculation, the result in dollars would be more gratifying at the end of the year. As it is, the majority of them are now losing money. It is a source of satisfaction, however, that these suggestions of mine which, I believe, are the first practical articles ever written on the subject of Tape Reading, have stirred the minds of many people to the possibilities in the line of scientific speculation.

This is shown in a number of letters I've received, many of them from traders situated in remote localities. In the main, the writers, who are now carrying on long distance operations for the big swings are desirous of testing their ability as Tape Readers. No doubt those who have written represent but a small percentage of the number who are thus inclined. To all such persons I would say you can make a success of Tape Reading but you must acquire a broad fundamental knowledge of the market. A professional singer who was recently called upon to advise a young aspirant said: "One must become a 'personality' - that is, an intelligence developed by the study of many things besides music". It is not enough to know a few of the underlying principles; one must have a deep understanding.

To be sure, it is possible for a person to take a number of the "tricks of the trade" herein mentioned and trade successfully on these alone. Even one idea which forms part of the whole subject may be worked and elaborated upon until it becomes a method in itself. There are endless possibilities in this direction, and after all it matters little how the money is extracted from the market, so long as it is done legitimately. But real Tape Reading takes everything into account - every little character which appears on the tape plays its part in forming one of the endless series of "moving pictures". In many years study of the tape, I do not remember having seen two of these "pictures" which were duplicates.

One can realize from this how impossible it would be to formulate a simple set of rules to fit every case or even the majority of them, as each 5 day trading session produces hundreds of situations, which, so far as memory serves, are never repeated. This goes on to suggest further that charts and chart 'pictures' are merely guides and cannot be relied upon to form judgments of the market at the moment you need it to.

The subject of Tape Reading is therefore practically inexhaustible, which makes it all the more interesting to the man who has acquired a habit of study. Having fortified himself with the necessary fundamental knowledge, the student of Tape Reading should thoroughly digest these suggestions and any others which may be obtainable in future. It is not enough to go over and over a lesson as a student in elementary school does, driving the facts into his head by monotonous repetition; tapes must be procured and the various indications matched up with what has been studied. And even after one believes he understands, he will presently learn that, to quote the words of a certain song, "You don't know how much you know until you know how little you know".

One of my instructors in another line of study used to make me go over a thing three or four times after I thought I knew it, just to make sure that I did.

I should say that it is almost impossible for one who has never before traded from the tape to go into a broker's office, start right in and operate successfully. In the first place, there are the abbreviations and all the little characters and their meanings to know, the abbreviations of the principal stocks; it is necessary to know everything that appears on the tape, so that nothing will be overlooked. Otherwise the trader will be like a person who attempts to read classic literature without knowing words of more than four letters.

It is a common impression that anyone who has the money can buy a seat on the Stock Exchange and at once begin making money as a floor trader. But floor trading is also a business that one has to learn, and it usually takes months and years to become accustomed to the physical and nervous strain and learn the ropes. Frequent requests are made for the name of someone who will teach the Art of Tape Reading. I do not know of anyone able to read the tape with profit who is willing to become an instructor.

The reason is very simple. Profits from the tape far exceed anything that might be earned by charging tuition fees to his students. It's simple economics. In addition to the large operators and floor traders who use Tape Reading in their daily work, there are a number of New York Stock Exchange members who never go on the floor, but spend the session at the ticker in their respective offices. Experience has taught them that they can produce larger profits by this method, or else they would not follow it.

The majority of them trade in 5000 share lots and up and their business forms an important share of the daily volume. A number of so-called semi-professionals operate on what may be termed pure 'intuitive' tape reading. They have no well-defined code of rules, methods or strategies and probably could not explain clearly just how they do it, but they "get the money" and that is the best proof of the pudding. The existence of even a comparatively small body of successful Tape Readers is evidence that money making by this means is an accomplished fact and should encourage you.

One of the greatest difficulties which the novice has to overcome is known as "cold feet". Too many people start and dabble a little without going far enough to determine whether or not they can make a go of it. And even those who get pretty well along in the subject will be scared to death at a string of losses and quit just when they should dig in harder. For in addition to learning the art they must form a sort of trading character, which no amount of reverses can discourage nor turn back and which constantly strives to eliminate its own weak points such as fear, greed, anxiety, nervousness and the many other mental factors which go to make or unmake the profits in this business. Perhaps I have painted a difficult proposition. If so, the greater will be the reward of those who master it. As stated at the beginning, Tape Reading is hard work. There seems no good reason for altering that opinion.

CHAPTER THIRTEEN

Two Days Trading - An Example Of My Method Applied

BELOW is a record of transactions made by me, results having been obtained by following the methods suggested in these pages on Tape Reading. The object is to show the possibilities in this adventure and to encourage anyone who wants to master the art of day trading.

Please note that out of fifteen transactions, figuring on the buying and selling prices alone, there were thirteen wins and only one loss. One transaction showed neither profit nor loss. Seven trades were on the long side and eight on the short. The stock fluctuated between 166 3/4 and 170 3/8 (3 5/8 points) during these two sessions, and gave numerous trading opportunities.

All transactions were protected by a close stop, in some cases not more than 1/8 or ¼ point from the original buying or selling price. These stop orders were not always put on the floor. The reason: in such active trading - stops could be changed or cancelled more quickly when they were carried in the head and executed "at the market" when the price hit the required figure.

Qty	Stock	Trade	Bought	Sold	Loss	Profit
200	Reading	Long	167 1/2	168 1/4		3/4
200	Reading	Short	167 1/4	168 3/8		1 1/8
200	Reading	Long	167 1/4	168 3/4		1 1/2
200	Reading	Short	169 5/8	169 3/4		1/8
200	Reading	Short	169	169 1/2		1/2
200	Reading	Short	169 1/8	170		7/8
100	Reading	Short	169 5/8	170		3/8
200	Reading	Short	168 1/8	169 7/8		1 3/4
200	Reading	Long	168	168		
200	Reading	Long	168 1/4	168 3/4		1/2
100	Reading	Short	168	169 1/4		1 1/4
100	Reading	Short	168 1/8	169 1/4		1 1/8
200	Reading	Long	168 1/8	168 1/2		3/8
200	Reading	Long	168 1/4	169		3/4
200	Reading	Short	169 1/4	168 3/8	7/8	
2700					7/8	11
	Commission				3 3/8	
	Tax (about)				1/4	
						-4 1/2
	Net Profits	(Points)				6 1/2

CHAPTER FOURTEEN

The Principles Applied to Longer Term Trading

THE first edition of this book having been exhausted, it has been my privilege to edit the foregoing chapters in preparation for the second edition. This has required a consideration of the principles therein set forth, and has enabled me to test and compare these principles in their adaptation to the stock market of 1916.

I find that in no important degree is it necessary to modify what has been written. While the character of the trading has altered since the outbreak of the European War, this change represents more a shifting of the leadership and a widening of the swings, due to extraordinary conditions. Proof that these rules and methods are correct is also found in their adaptation to other forms of trading, chief among which is the detection of accumulation and distribution at certain important turning points in the market. I have used this method successfully in forecasting the market for these principal swings and find it to be a much more comfortable way of following the market, because it is not so confining.

Preparation for a long advance or decline, as well as for the intermediate movements are numerous, is clearly apparent to those who understand the art of Tape Reading. In judging the market by its own action, it is unimportant whether you are endeavouring to forecast the next small half hourly swing or the trend for the next two or three weeks. The same indications as to price, volume, activity, support and pressure, are exhibited in the preparation for both. The same elements will be found in a drop of water as in the ocean, and vice versa. A study of the stock market means a study in the forces above and below the present level of prices. Each movement has its period of preparation, execution and termination, and the most substantial of movements are those that make long preparation. Without this preparation and gathering of force, a movement is not likely to be sustained.

On the other hand, the greater the preparation, the greater the probable extent of the swing. Preparation for the principal movements in the market will very often occupy several months. This may be preceded by a decline, in which large operators accumulate their stocks. They may even precipitate this decline in order to pave the way for such accumulation.

Large operators differ from small ones in their ability to foresee important changes in stock market values from six months to a year in advance, and to prepare themselves for it. A study of these preparatory periods discloses to those who understand the anatomy of market movements the direction and possible extent of the next big move. Thus, a study of these important turning points, principal among which are booms and panics, is the most essential. Small operators should take a leaf from the book of those who buy and sell enormous quantities of securities. It is their foresight which enables them to profit.

To cultivate foresight means to study the markets condition. In a lecture at the Finance Forum, New York, I showed how all influences of every sort affecting the stock market are shown on the tape, and in the changes in prices. While I would not for a moment discourage the student from acquiring any knowledge, and giving some consideration to Fundamental Statistics such as crops, money, politics, corporate earnings, etc.- the advantages of studying the action of the market, as a guide to future prices, are productive of too great results to warrant their dilution with factors which are really of secondary importance. I make this claim because of my conviction that the position of large operators is more important than the so-called basic factors.

For several years past I have applied the principles in this book to the forecasting of the swings of from 5 to 20 points. Results have been highly outstanding. For this reason I can recommend that the subject be studied with a view to the formation of a method of trading, especially adapted to the individual requirements of those who wish to follow this intensely interesting and highly profitable business.

R I C H A R D   D .   W Y C K O F F
New York, 1919

www.ingramcontent.com/pod-product-compliance
Lightning Source LLC
Chambersburg PA
CBHW060042210326
41520CB00009B/1227